Praise for

Writing Secrets: Essential Steps to Discover How to Start

"*Writing Secrets: Essential Steps to Discover How to Start* is a gift to future authors everywhere. Any of us who have already written a book wish that we'd read Tim Morrison's book before we got started! Tim not only demystifies the process of writing, but empowers readers with a practical road map to make the book of your dreams come true. He is both mentor and dream-maker as he guides you to trust your heart and develop your own writing voice as you bring your project to life. If you have an idea for a book you want to write and need to know how to get it done, you've come to the 'write' place. Stop right now and read this book!"

Mike Pniewski, Actor, Speaker, Author of When Life Gives You Lemons, Throw 'em Back!

"Tim Morrison's *Writing Secrets: Essential Steps to Discover How to Start* will erase every fear and doubt you have ever had about writing your first book. Leaving no stone unturned, Tim leads the first-time author step-by-step through the entire writing process—from releasing the emotional roadblocks that may be keeping you from sharing your genius with the world to the polishing of your first literary gem! A must-read for everyone who wants to unleash their inner-author!"

Heather K. O'Hara, Award-winning Poet & Author, Founder & CEO, Watermark Publishing

"Writing is indeed a profound and powerful journey, and Tim Morrison's excellent book will be an enormously helpful guide to you as you embark on that sacred journey of discovery and sharing of the gifts of your own words of wisdom with others. This book will help you clarify your message, allow you to ask the deep questions that will fuel your writing journey, and inspire you to keep going along the way, even at times when it may be difficult. Tim has a unique, deep, spiritual perspective on the writing process, and as you move through each chapter of this book, you will feel that you are being guided by a warm, wise, wonderful writerly friend, who will inspire you to new levels of comfort, confidence and creativity as your words begin to flow."

Caroline Joy Adams Author of The Power to Write, Public Speaker and Writing Coach

"Great overall advice. I like the step-by-step flow."

Renée Walkup, SalesPEAK, Inc., Author of "Selling to Anyone Over the Phone"
www.salespeak.com

Praise for

Writing Secrets: Essential Steps to Discover How to Start

"Writing can be a very daunting, confusing, complicated process, and so can reading books about writing. This is by far the most accessible, straight-forward, practical book that I have read on the subject."

Emily Lees, public high school English teacher and an MFA candidate in creative nonfiction

"I wish I had the opportunity to read Tim Morrison's book when I decided to become an author. I would have saved a lot of time and energy that was wasted on figuring it out for myself. It's never easy to write a book, but Tim makes it much more fun and rewarding."

Tricia Molloy, Author of Divine Wisdom at Work:
10 Universal Principles for Enlightened Entrepreneurs

"I so wish I had had a book like *Writing Secrets: Essential Steps to Discover How to Start* when I began writing. The clear examples from the author's own experience and others he writes about show his compassion for the writer who is just getting started — while also giving excellent ideas for how to think about writing and how to plumb one's own depths to discover and then write about one's topic. This book is a terrific contribution to the world of books about writing."

Lorna McLeod, Lead Coach, The Leading Mentors Publishing and Marketing Program

"A friendly, well-organized and thorough primer on how to move beyond basic barriers to writing that we all have from our school days and solid information on how to find the topic that we can put our hearts and minds into writing about."

Nadia Prisuta, English Teacher, Sharpsville Area School District, PA

"Tim Morrison found ways to approach the process differently. Drawing on old journals is especially clever – the freewriting is done – which brings the writer to the next task – finding a topic from the freewrite. *Lectio divina* is great – it gives structure to the process of finding a topic. The book comes at both of these challenging steps in the process with a fresh perspective and pragmatic approaches for getting through them. I've read a lot of books on writing, and what I appreciate about this book is that it addresses these two steps in an accessible way."

Paula Miller, College of Wooster Writing Center Intern,
The University of Akron – Graduate Teaching Assistant

Praise for

Writing Secrets: Essential Steps to Discover How to Start

"Tim Morrison has a lot of good thoughts that are well organized. This book *Writing Secrets: Essential Steps to Discover How to Start* provides practical advice and insight on how to get focused and started."

Mary Branson, author

"I found the work to be very engaging, and it certainly kept my interest."

Pete Geiger, Philom., Editor, Farmers' Almanac

"I think the application of the lectio divina to the writing process is remarkable. Tim Morrison's explanation of the process is crystal clear and his application of it to the writing process is superb."

Jill Jepson, Author of Writing as a Sacred Path, transformational writing coach

"Dr. Morrison adeptly combines writing from his heart and mind and shows you how to do the same. In doing so you awaken the writer within you. His book provides you practical insight and steps to take to clarify what you want to say and how to best articulate your topic. You will be inspired to take action on your dream and get going on your 'someday' book today."

Pat Fiorello, Fiorello Art & Design, LLC

"Quite a bit of information and materials pass over my desk. I found what you shared to be a very good read with helpful information for anyone serious about writing."

Norma Saken, assistant to Lee Iacocca

"To succeed at writing, you must first give yourself *Permission to Succeed*. Tim shows you how to write from the heart and touch your core audience. Use this book and awaken the writer within you."

Noah St. John, author of The Secret Code of Success and inventor of Afformations

Also by

Tim Morrison

A Walk in the Spirit:
Creating Dramatic Monologues through Lectio Divina

Letters To My Sons: a Father's Faith Journey

Healing Plants of the Bible: Then and Now

Available through:
www.BarnesandNoble.com

Writing SECRETS

Essential Steps to Discover How to Start

by **Tim Morrison**

AXIS
PUBLISHING & DISTRIBUTION COMPANY, LLC
Huntsville, Alabama

First Edition Printed, 2010

Published by:
Axis Publishing & Distribution Company, LLC
4500 Campus Drive, STE #488
Newport Beach, CA 92660
Email: info@axis-publishing.com
Website: www.Axis-Publishing.com

Cover Art and Layout Design by: Vanessa Lowry

Axis Publishing & Distribution Company books may be purchased in bulk for educational, business, fundraising or sales promotional use. For information please write:

Special Markets Department, Axis Publishing & Distribution Company, LLC,
4500 Campus Drive, STE #488, Newport Beach, CA 92660.
Email: SpecialMarkets@Axis-Publishing.com

This book is sold with the understanding that neither the publisher nor the author(s) are engaging in, nor rendering legal, medical, psychiatric, accounting or any other professional service. If you need legal, accounting, medical, psychiatric or other expert advice, then you should seek the services of a duly licensed professional.

Library of Congress Control Number: 2010934813
ISBN: 978-0-9822479-2-1

Printed in the United States of America

To Marta
Celebrating 20 wonderful years
and
looking forward to many more

Acknowledgements

I am grateful to Janet Litherland Barnes for her continued enthusiasm and encouragement of my writing as she edits my drafts into even better material.

I extend a heartfelt thank you to Don West, Jr and Axis Publishing and to Ahmad Meradji and BookLogix.

Thank you to Vanessa Lowry, cover design artist and layout. You did an absolutely amazing job!

I also thank the following people for their helpful and insightful reading of the manuscript:

Caroline Joy Adams	Lorna McCleod
Mary Branson	Paula Miller
Terri Defilipp	Ivan Misner
Richelle Dowdell	Tricia Molloy
Pat Fiorello	Joel Morrison
Pete Geiger	Marta Morrison
Julie Grace	Heather K. O'Hara
Mary Theresa Hall	Emile Paradis
Jill Jepson	Mike Pniewski
John Kohari	Nadia Prisuta
Rob Krock	Noah St. John
Emily Lees	Norma Saken
Harry Levinson	Renee Walkup
Linda Masek	Lisa Zunzanyika

To the literally hundreds of individuals who responded to the polls that I sent out, thank you for taking the time to respond.

T.M.

Foreword

Doubt and uncertainty envelop many writers as they contemplate their lifelong ambition of writing a book. Many writers start simply with essays, journals, and short stories, hoping that these small steps will aid in their quest to produce enough pages to compile a book.

I've rejected numerous articles because the writer strayed beyond the subject — unable to focus on the topic. I've read many fiction contest entries that go on and on boring the reader. Why? The writer couldn't develop one plot, but instead, tried to take on too much, too many subplots.

Before writers can begin the first page of the book they must know what to write about. Sounds simple and logical enough, but is it? I want to write about family tragedies. Commendable as that topic might be, the writer needs to be able to put family tragedies into words. But when it comes down to putting emotions and memories into a book-length form, the once determined writer may fall short. Should I tell all? Who shouldn't I refer to? Should I keep things lighthearted? or serious?

Knowing what you are writing about will help you market and sell your book. No publisher will be interested in your book if a clear defined subject isn't covered.

Where to begin? Here, with the book you are holding.

Tim Morrison's years as a writing coach have helped him produce a handbook for anyone considering the challenge of writing a book — any book. His *Lectio Divina* process of determining what to write about helps writers focus. Instead of questioning what to write about and how to write the book, readers of this book will know what to write.

Or use a mind-mapping process Morrison outlines to help define the focus of your work. The novice book writer hell-bent on producing a volume of words may become discouraged when the many topics and subtopics present their ugly heads.

Writing a book is an awesome accomplishment that only those with strong perseverance and fortitude will achieve. So read this book before you begin writing a book because this book gives you the tools to help you decide what your book will be about.

Leon Ogroske, Editor, WRITERS' Journal

Your life is a sacred journey. And it is about change, growth, discovery, movement, transformation, continuously expanding your vision of what is possible, stretching your soul, learning to see clearly and deeply, listening to your intuition, taking courageous challenges at every step along the way. You are on the path . . . exactly where you are meant to be right now . . . And from here, you can only go forward, shaping your life story into a magnificent tale of triumph, of healing, of courage, of beauty, of wisdom, of power, of dignity, and of love.

~ Caroline Joy Adams

Table of Contents

Introduction

Someday . . .

Remember the time you told your friends about an amazing adventure you had on a recent vacation? Then there was that time you attended a major conference where people gathered from all across the nation. At the end of a day, you sat with colleagues old and new and everyone shared thoughts on what the various speakers had said during their presentations. How about the holiday family gathering from a couple of years ago? You easily recall that time. Stories abounded about Great-Aunt Ruth or Uncle Bill or Cousin Ken. Then you reminisced about Grandma Liz. Your tales brought the most laughter, comments and questions. In each of these situations, someone challenged you, "You should write a book!" And you answered – or wanted to answer, "I think I will someday."

You did think about it – writing that book about adventures you've had in your life; or that book in which you offer insights into a profession that others find to be so fascinating. Perhaps your book will share stories that you learned over a lifetime about your extended family. What about the book that has always churned within you. You have thought about it and you have told yourself time and again – someday. But "someday" continues to elude you.

Twice during my elementary school days I dreamed of being an author. The first time I thought about writing a book was on a hot summer day when I was ten years old. I was staying with my cousin for a few days and on the spur of the moment we decided that we each would write a book – a best seller of course – starting right now! We grabbed pencils and tablets, dashed out to the front porch where there was a bit of a cool breeze and began to write. No planning, just writing. Our pencils flew across the lines on our tablets. We labored with excitement and anticipation. After what seemed like an eternity, I looked at my watch: 15 minutes had gone by and I had written one page. Clearly this was going to take a lot longer than I had anticipated. My cousin and I looked at each other, glanced at our tablets, and laughed. We dropped our pencils and tablets on the porch floor and ran off to play. So much for that "someday."

My second brush with writing came in sixth grade. Each student in the class was to choose a country, research its history, write a six- or seven-page report on that country, then give an oral presentation to the class. I chose Brazil. I started my research at the small public library in my home town, where I found books and articles on Brazil. Next I wrote to the Brazilian embassy in Washington, DC, and to the Brazilian ambassador to the United Nations. Those letters generated an amazing amount of materials including information on the creation and construction of the new capital city of Brasilia. As I wrote my paper, an idea began to formulate in my mind.

All the books that I had used for research had been written by adults. Each contained a wealth of information, maybe even too much information from my perspective. What would it have been like to find a book written for kids by kids?

I began to think: There were 30 students in my class. Each of us had to write a report on a country. Some countries were chosen by more than one student. Not all of the reports would be of high quality. But if I could get 15 or 20 reports, I would have a book written by kids for kids.

I knew nothing about the publishing world. I had never heard of agents or query letters. I simply had what I believed to be a great idea – and I decided to act. I didn't ask my parents or my teacher how to go about getting published. Instead, I looked at the books I used in my research and determined what publishing house had published most of them or at least several of them. It seemed to me that if one publisher showed an interest in publishing a particular kind of book, then that publisher would surely be interested in my proposal. Good reasoning for not really knowing what I was doing!

In my letter I shared that I was a sixth grader and that our teacher had given us an assignment to do research and write a report on a country. I had discovered in doing my research on Brazil that this publishing house had published several of the books that I had used. I had spoken with some of my classmates about their papers and research, and they too had used a number of books by the same publisher. Clearly the publisher had an interest in this field. I suggested that we could provide a unique opportunity for the publisher to come out with a new book from a different perspective: a book written by students for students. I wrote that I was certain I could get at least 15 high-quality reports. I shared what countries I believed those reports would represent with Brazil leading the way. I sent my letter and waited.

Several weeks passed. I came home from school one day and found a letter addressed to me lying on the family room table. The return address was embossed with the publishing company's name. I tore open the letter. This was going to be the start of an exciting adventure. Instead, the adventure came to a screeching halt. This was what decades later I came to know as a rejection letter. What I didn't realize then was that it was not the standard form letter used for rejections. This was a personal letter, typewritten and signed by the acquisitions editor himself. He commended me on my idea, proposal, creative thinking and suggestion. However, the company could not fit the book concept in with its publication schedule at that time. A couple of handwritten lines followed in which the acquisitions editor encouraged me to hold onto my dream of writing a book.

Looking back on that experience, I chuckle over my naïveté: thinking that a major publisher would consider a manuscript from an elementary school student. I imagine my letter was handwritten on notebook paper. But the acquisitions editor took the time to respond personally and to give encouragement to this sixth-grade student. With that, my adventure as a writer seeking to be published ended at least for the next forty years.

In 1993, Meriwether Publishing released *Everything New and Who's Who in Clown Ministry* by Janet Litherland. I was one of 21 clowns featured in the book. (I had been involved in clown ministry for over 10 years.) Janet invited me to appear in my clown persona for a book signing event. We had shared correspondence and telephone conversations over the preceding six years, but we had not seen each other for nearly 30 years when she had been my high school chorus and speech teacher. When the book signing event ended and I got out of clown make-up, we met for lunch and conversation. Janet asked me if I had ever prepared and preached a certain type of sermon – at that time I was a parish pastor and had been in ministry for nearly 20 years. I answered by asking her how many she had in mind, as I had many sermons in the form of a dramatic monologue.

"Do you have about twenty?"

"Yes, I do."

"Then let's put them together and get them published!"

"Published? As in a book published?

"Yes."

"You are serious, aren't you?"

"Yes, I am. I will work with you. Haven't you ever thought about writing a book someday?"

And then I remembered that summer afternoon when I was ten . . . and my idea in sixth grade that prompted an encouraging rejection letter from an editor.

"Yes, I have."

It would be great to write that Janet and I were successful; that once we got the manuscript together and sent it off to several publishers for consideration, I was published. But that is not what happened. Over the next 13 years, I did two extensive rewrites and reformatting of the manuscript. I accumulated 27 rejection letters. Finally in 2008, the manuscript was published. *A Walk in the Spirit* became not my first but my third published book.

How frequently do you think about writing a book? You dream of seeing your name in print as the author of a book. In your mind you see your book listed on Amazon.com and watch as your friends, relatives and the general public flood online to order the book. You see your name and book on the *New York Times* best seller list.

Then reality takes over. You ask yourself, "What am I thinking?" But the subtle echo in your mind persists: Someday, someday, someday. What holds you back? What keeps you from tackling that dream?

I have some thoughts on that which emerge from my own writing history. During my 25+ years in ministry, I wrote sermons, newsletter articles, curricula, devotional booklets, short dramas, seminar content and a host of articles that appeared in national publications. After leaving ministry, I worked for 4 years as a naturopathic counselor and wrote 3 booklets to assist my clients in their journeys to "better well-being." Also as a naturopathic counselor, I wrote and had published my first book – *Healing Plants of the Bible: Then and Now.* In 2005, I joined Write Choice Services as a writing coach and subsequently bought the company when the founder/ owner decided to retire. From those vast and various writing experiences and from my work as a writing coach, I have generated ideas on what I believe are basic barriers that prevent people from writing their "someday" book. This is my fourth book. I've co-authored a book on legacy writing with Don West, Jr., and we are working on a sequel to that one. I want you to benefit from my experience so that your "someday" will happen. Here is a preview of what you will find in the chapters ahead:

CHAPTER 1: *School Days, Good Old Fashioned Rule Days* discusses the basic barriers that stand in the way of writing.

CHAPTER 2: *Good Is Good Enough* probes a question that gets asked frequently in writing seminars and workshops. Can people learn to be good, better, great writers?

CHAPTER 3: *Seven Solid Benefits from Writing a Book* provides encouragement for the emerging writer. Here I help you recognize a variety of substantive reasons for engaging in writing a book and the benefits that may accrue.

CHAPTER 4: *What I Know or What I Don't Know?* addresses another issue frequently raised by aspiring writers, first time writers: what should I write about?

CHAPTER 5: *What to Do with All My Notes and Journals* offers insights on how to use the notes, journals, and diaries that you have written over the years.

The next three chapters are the heart of this book. Books abound that provide step-by-step directions on how to write your book, even on how to write your book in 30 days or in a weekend. Regardless of your theme or genre, you can find at least one book that will guide you through the process of writing fiction, nonfiction, memoir, advice, how-to books. These books assume that you already know your topic. Many of my clients come to me with several possible topics and they want to know which one would be best to develop a book around. Or they wonder if they do in fact have several book topics or can their thoughts be compiled into one solid book. Chapters 6, 7 and 8 will lead you on that discovery journey. Once you master the material in those chapters, you should be able to approach the other "how to write a book" books with significant confidence.

CHAPTER 6: *The Secret to Finding Your Book Topic* introduces a centuries-old process known as *Lectio Divina*. Don't let the Latin name generate anxiety. The process has worked with my clients every time. I've personally used it for decades to help me center in on a writing topic or book topic.

CHAPTER 7: *Mind Mapping Your Book* shows you how to take your discoveries from Chapter 6's process and build upon them, taking the next step in writing your book.

CHAPTER 8: *Sharpening Your Focus* assists you in identifying information that will guide you in maintaining focus as you write.

CHAPTER 9: *Reading and Writing Go Together* encourages you to see the critical connection between writing and reading. Reading strengthens writing, while writing often triggers a hunger to read.

CHAPTER 10: *Finding Your Writing Voice* acquaints you with the concept of the writing voice: why it is important; how to develop one.

CHAPTER 11: *Writing as an Act of Discovery, Reverence and Sacred Trust* suggests that writing is more than storytelling. Writing has a spiritual dimension. This chapter discusses ways to approach writing so that you will write the best that you have to share.

CHAPTER 12: *Now to Begin* provides thoughts on "where to go from here" along with some final thoughts on writing.

APPENDIX: I want to draw attention to an entry in the appendix – prints of 2 types of labyrinths. Labyrinths have been an integral part of my writing journey. A labyrinth can help you overcome writer's block, focus your thinking and unleash your creativity.

This book invites you on a journey to discover and express the writer within you. I believe that this journey is a sacred journey. It is the type of journey that Caroline Joy Adams describes in this book's epigraph: ". . . it is about change, growth, discovery, movement, transformation, continuously expanding your vision of what is possible, stretching your soul, learning to see clearly and deeply, listening to your intuition, taking courageous challenges at every step along the way."

Enjoy the journey.

I encourage you to walk a labyrinth printed in the appendix or check out **www.labyrinths.org** to see if there is a labyrinth in your area that you could actually walk. Share with me your labyrinth experiences and writing. Send me an e-mail: **stories@writechoiceservices.com**. Put **labyrinth stories** as the subject.

Have a tenderness and determination toward your writing, a sense of humor and a deep patience that you are doing the right thing. ~ Natalie Goldberg

Chapter 1

School Days, Good Old Fashioned Rule Days

In writing, you explore what it means to be you: who you are as a business person, speaker, spouse, educator, dreamer, writer, parent, or entrepreneur. Through your writing, you share with others what it means to see the world as you see it. That is what happens when in conversation you have shared a story or reflected upon an event, and then someone challenges you with those intriguing words: You ought to write a book. Your view of the world, whether that is your world of work or life or parenting or something else, brought a new perspective, a new understanding to at least one person. In writing you take that perspective to a wider audience.

My own writing experience as well as the writing experiences of those with whom I have worked suggests that four basic barriers keep folks from picking up a pen and starting to write. They are: 1) memories from school; 2) writing topic uncertainty; 3) finding time to write; 4) friends, colleagues, and family.

What memories flood your mind when you think of the essays and term papers you wrote in your high school days? If your memories are similar to mine, then they are not pleasant. I can still feel the knot in my stomach that appeared each time a teacher gave an essay assignment. At home, at my desk, beginning my homework, I often felt the sting of tears welling in my eyes as I thought about the topic. Where did these ideas come from? Compare and contrast this book with that one. What are the three main themes in the novel and how does the author use those themes to move the plot along? What did Shakespeare have in mind when he wrote . . . and how does this appear in the play/sonnet?

Occasionally the teacher would challenge us with, "Share your opinion on . . . Write what you believe to be true or arguable but back up your words with sources." That was a bit easier. We did our research. We formulated our thoughts. We gave written response, defending our position. With high expectations, we turned in those papers.

How often did the essays come back with rivers of red ink on the pages? The teacher wrote comments, made corrections and posted a grade at the top. Maybe we didn't have a whole lot of red ink on our papers but the memories of the struggles experienced in writing remain if only subconsciously.

Remember your College Freshman English Composition course? The themes assigned by the professor made those of your high school teachers seem ridiculously easy. Then you spent late nights or even all-nighters to meet deadlines. Despite your best intention and efforts, the papers returned with the same amount of red ink, maybe even more red ink.

What about length? In high school, you struggled to write a five-page paper. A couple of times, you had to write term papers that were 15 or 20 pages in length. College was the same thing only course papers could easily be 10 pages long. Research papers, honors papers, and senior thesis required 25 pages as a minimum. You wrestled to write those papers. And those essays and themes and papers were required for graduation. How can you ever manage to write a 125-page manuscript? "But someday." You said it out loud. You've said it to yourself.

Dig deeper into our memories and we encounter the horrors of grammar and punctuation rules, spelling lists to be memorized, sentences to diagram. Misspelled words, improper punctuation and the shattering of grammar generated a lot of the red ink on your essays, themes and term projects. You are not much better now than you were then. In fact with the passage of years, you may be even more challenged with proper grammar and spelling. Spell-check helps but it can't catch everything.

Even worse, you might have had one of those nightmarish teachers who told you directly and clearly that you would never be a writer. You believed the teacher. Even when you began to get less red ink and more insightful comments on your writing, the dismissive words of the disquieting teacher still held center place in your mind.

Such memories hinder our willingness to take the plunge into the writing world. We can't see beyond what once was. But we need to move beyond those memories. The situation is different now. You are no longer in high school or college. You get to pick your writing topic. The only red ink you will experience will be from your own pen or that of your friends, relatives and peers whom you have invited to read and comment on your manuscript. Moreover, you have a story to tell, an adult parable or children's story to share, or a business insight that others could benefit from.

This is now. Your spoken words have already touched an individual – the one who told you that you ought to write a book. There are those who want to experience your view of the world. There is no grading, just writing the manuscript to your own specifications. You can do this. Really!

The second barrier is finding clarity on a writing topic. As the title suggests and as I confirmed in the introduction, finding a book topic is the focus of this book. First, however, there are attending issues to address.

Remember the "someday" moments. What had you shared? What were you discussing that prompted the "you ought to write a book" challenge? That is a beginning point for your determining a topic or a theme at the very least.

You have concern that what you share will not be new or truly unique. That is all right. Check out the bibliography of this book. It is but a sampling of the books available on writing. These are only the ones I used in researching this book. Go to your favorite book store and find the section that carries the category or genre of book you would like to write. Look at all the titles you find in that section. Does any book in that section address the topic as you would? Read the synopsis on the back cover. Glance at the table of contents. Skim over the preface or introduction. I think you will find that although some similarities may exist between each of these books' approach and yours, your book will put it all together in one volume instead of in several.

Choose an online book store/dealer and do the same thing. Enter the genre or category, click on search, sit back and review all the results.

Natalie Goldberg comments: "A writer's job is to make the ordinary come alive, to awaken ourselves to the specialness of simply being . . . Learn to write about the ordinary. Give homage to old coffee cups, sparrows, city buses, thin ham sandwiches." Her words hold true, regardless of your topic. Nuclear physicists, rocket scientists and parents are always looking for a new perspective on the ordinary in their fields.

You do not necessarily want to be the first writer in a new field. There is no history on how that field will play; no solid, identifiable market. That is a bit risky for a first-book, first-time writer.

You want to write because you believe you have a different spin on things. You take a different slant on work issues, policy matters, how to do something. You have something valid to share.

My first book, *Healing Plants of the Bible: Then and Now*, began as a dissertation. I had not given any thought to having it published. I shared my dissertation with Dr. Andrew Linial, colleague and friend, and he encouraged me to seek publication. So, I took the plunge. (This was 6 years and 18 rejection letters into the 13 years and 27 rejection letters of trying to get my dramatic monologue book published.)

I kept encountering individuals who wanted to use alternative medicine but they had been told that such things were pagan or a tool of the devil. I had left ministry after 25 years and was now a part of the alternative medical field.

For three years of my 25-plus years in ministry, I had lived in a bush village in Ghana. Frequently when illness or discomfort arose, the only recourse any of us in the village had for getting relief or a cure was to turn to herbalists – what we in the West refer to as alternative medicine. (Ironically, what we call alternative medicine is labeled traditional medicine for many people in the world.) It did not make sense to me to describe something as pagan or as a tool of the devil simply because it was different from mainstream, Western medicine. Through research, I discovered numerous books on plants of the Bible and healing plants but there was very little written on healing plants of the Bible. Additionally, I found very little mention of theological perspectives on plants used for healing that are mentioned in the Bible. That would be my niche.

I addressed those concepts, added the chapters to my dissertation and found a publisher. I combined my background and experience as an ordained minister and educator with my practical experience of living in a bush village combined with my new knowledge of naturopathy to generate a book that would help people of faith see that alternative medicine was certainly not pagan nor a tool of the devil.

The third reason or barrier named by folks who want to write but don't is time – how to find the time to write amidst a life that is most likely already overscheduled. The simple answer is: change your perspective and you will find the time. Even successful authors and individuals who write full time do not devote eight hours a day to writing.

In her comments on writing, Anne Lamott declares, "Write your 300 words then go for a walk." Four pages, double spaced, typewritten or about 1,000 words is a common daily goal. Some writers set a page goal while others set a word goal. Figure out what makes sense to you, what feels comfortable and what is attainable.

Writing can be a slow process. Greg Ames worked for five years on his debut book, *Buffalo Lockjaw*, which won the 2009 New Atlantic Independent Booksellers Association award for Trade Paperback Original. In 2002 Therese Walsh, who is the co-founder of Writer Unboxed, a blog for writers about the craft and business of genre fiction, began writing a story. In 2005, she chucked the entire thing and started over. She aimed her story line toward a different genre. Walsh's book, *The Last Will of Moira Leahy*, was published in 2009. In my own writing, each of my books required about six months from conception to completed manuscript.

Several factors effect the length of time needed to complete a manuscript: your knowledge of the subject or topic; research you may have to do; the time you devote to writing daily or weekly; your own motivation and confidence. Marathon writers do exist and literally thousands of individuals participate in the annual NaNoWriMo – National Novel Writing Month – which is November. The website for this adventure is www.nanowrimo.org. Book stores and online booksellers offer a variety of books on "how to write a book in a month" or a week or even in a weekend. You may want to look at some of those books to learn what each suggests as the critical components for completing a writing project in a set time frame.

Ultimately, successfully writing a book "someday" comes down to finding actual writing time. How do we do that in our tightly scheduled lives? By being creative is the best answer. Samantha Wilde, author of *This Little Mommy Stayed Home*, initially wrote during her son's naps.

Now she hires a baby sitter for four to eight hours a week. *Rivet Head*, the story of a "shop rat" on an assembly line, was written by Ben Hamper during his breaks from the assembly line and in evenings after work. Aspiring authors write on coffee breaks and lunch breaks. They get up an hour earlier and write before going to work or before taking on the day. Some write late at night. A few get up in the dead of night, when family members are asleep, and write. A few snatch a weekend away in a motel or lodge or cabin.

If you want to write, then discipline yourself. Set aside blocks of time to write. Those blocks may be short – 15 minutes, lunch break, just before going to bed. They may be longer – an hour for two mornings a week, a couple of hours each weekend. Some time is indeed better than no time and wishful thinking. Get started.

In the meantime, keep a notebook handy or stash index cards in your purse, pocket or day planner so you can jot down notes, or ideas when they come to mind. Flesh them out later.

Finally the fourth barrier: people! This could be friends, co-workers, family, spouse. It seems curious to suggest people as a barrier, especially since I have suggested that individuals have been the source of encouragement for you to write. The barrier is more self-generated as we allow ourselves to worry about "what will people think" when we tell them we are writing a book. Specifically, will they laugh?

You will find no rule in writing that requires you to tell anyone that you are writing a manuscript. But, if you do tell others, you will most likely find them to be intrigued and excited. They will want to know your topic and when your book will be available. They may ask, "Can I have an autographed copy when it comes out?" They may also share with you their secret desire to write a book as well.

Remember that through words, you can share with others what it means to see the world as you see it and experience it. Only you can share your take on the world, on business, on the future, on some adventure. Only you can share the stories and perspectives that lie within you.

This chapter began with a quotation from Natalie Goldberg. I want to close this chapter by sharing the rest of Goldberg's comment. "Have a tenderness and determination toward your writing, a sense of humor and a deep patience that you are doing the right thing. Avoid getting caught by that small gnawing mouse of doubt. See beyond it to the vastness of life and the belief in time and practice."

Don't get caught by doubt. Don't let simple barriers hold you back. See beyond the doubt and barriers to the power of the words you have to share.

I am interested in hearing your "red ink syndrome" stories and your memories associated with writing high school essays and college papers. E-mail your stories to: **stories@writechoiceservices.com**.
Put **red ink** in the subject line.

Progress, not perfection.
~*Joel Saltzman, based on the teachings of Alcoholics Anonymous*

Chapter 2

Good Is
Good Enough

You are ready to tackle the keyboard or pick up a pen. You are poised to write. Then a voice inside you tells you, "Your writing is not that great." Foolishly, you listen to the voice. What do you do about that voice? Is it all right simply to be an "okay writer?"

Consider the number of books available today. Now, expand that perspective. Imagine all of the books that have ever been published and marketed. How many have been dubbed great? Relatively speaking, comparatively few. The majority of books are simply good. They inform. They entertain. They offer a new spin on an idea or process or story line.

Writers do dream of creating the next great International novel or having the next *New York Times'* best seller on the self-help or nonfiction lists. We all have dreams, regardless of our profession. What writers understand is that "good" works. Good writing is acceptable writing. Bookstores and our personal libraries are filled with well-written, good books.

That voice we hear is a barrier in disguise. That voice recalls the red ink syndrome. Ignore the voice. Remember your mission. You have a story to tell, a legacy to share. You have a different perspective on a practice or process in your profession. You have ideas that will help others. Natalie Goldberg, in *Writing Down the Bones*, encourages writers: "If you are not afraid of the voices inside you, you will not fear the critics outside of you . . . You can explain with deep knowledge what it means to be [you]. . . You know it better than anyone else."

Write your story. Share your insight!

Is writing teachable? Can you become a better writer or improve your writing style?

If writing isn't teachable, then we are wasting a lot of tax dollars and tuition money on English courses in the public schools, private schools, colleges and universities. We learn the rules of grammar and punctuation, proper word usage, sentence structure, parts of speech and paragraph formation in the English classes of grade school, secondary school and undergraduate studies. We struggle through myriad essays set before us each year with none being more challenging than the indefatigable required College Freshman English Composition course.

But those are simply the mechanics of writing, you may argue. You are absolutely correct; however, until you have mastered the mechanics of the written language, you will be challenged to express yourself clearly in written form. That is the stuff of the English classes of our basic educational journey.

Because we learn about grammar, voice, point of view, elements of style, we are also able to read what others write because those writers understand and use the rules of grammar, voice, point of view. It is a simple yet profound truth that should give you encouragement to write.

Some high schools offer creative writing classes. In colleges, universities and adult learning centers, you can find a variety of writing courses. An internet search or paging through writing magazines will uncover workshops on writing, summer writing institutes and writing coaches to help improve your writing. You will find online courses as well. Go to the writing section in any book store. Discover the abundant variety of "how to" books on writing.

A lot of school administrators, teachers and writers clearly believe it is possible to help writers write better. And I number myself among them.

I chuckle each time I think about Anne Lamott's comment on teaching writing. You can find it in her book, *Bird by Bird*: "But you can't teach writing, people tell me. And I say, 'Who . . . are you, God's dean of admissions?' If people show up in one of my classes and want to learn to write or to write better, I can tell them everything that has helped me along the way and what it is like for me on a daily basis. I can teach them little things that may not be in any of the great books on writing."

Sometimes when individuals ask, "Can you teach people to write," the question behind the question is, "Can you teach people to become great writers or best-selling authors?" There is a difference. There is also a difference between writing and being published. And there is a difference between being published and making a sustainable income from being published.

My focus in this book is to get you writing. You have an idea or several ideas you want to write about, but barriers hold you back. I will help you attack those barriers and give you guidance on getting focused on a topic.

Turning to Stephen King *On Writing* ". . . while it is impossible to make a competent writer out of a bad writer . . . it is possible with lots of hard work, dedication and timely help to make a good writer out of a merely competent one." I read those words as encouragement.

Several years ago, I found an interesting comment on the website of a book doctor/writing coach. He said that if great writing were teachable then every M.A. or PhD in English would be a best-selling author! We know that has not happened. Notice though, the individual's qualifier – "great writing." Good writing, or as Stephen King describes it, competent writing, is good enough.

You can do it! You have a story to tell, an idea to share, a business point to make. You have your unique viewpoint on the world, an amazing family history or a compilation of events that always generates laughter. Good. Go for it! Write! But do so with a nod to reality laced with determination.

In the preface of my book, *Letters to My Sons: a Father's Faith Journey*, I begin with this paragraph: "If, as you read this book, you find yourself saying, 'I could have written this,' then I am on the way to attaining my goal. If you actually take time to sit down and write your journey for your children . . . then I have truly succeeded with my intention for this book." I knew my writing was good. I hoped that some readers might experience it as great. But it was good enough and I truly hoped that others would be motivated to write similar reflections because of how I wrote.

Consider the kind of writing you have been doing over the years. Are you responsible for quarterly reports? Annual reports? Do you write daily or weekly memos? Are you responsible for directives? How often do you write or have you written letters? Maybe you have submitted something to your faith community's newsletter or your company's in-house publication.

Do you blog? Keep journals? Have a diary? Write Christmas letters? Have you written down events from your childhood to share with your children or grandchildren? Are you surprised to discover all of the writing that you engage in? You just saw it as part of your work, your family obligation, something you volunteer to do. Take a moment to recall some of the excitement you have experienced as you crafted words to convey an image or a word picture. Think about it. Are you now smiling because you realize that you have on occasion put together a string of words or ideas that sounded a bit like music?

What have others told you about your reports? Your Christmas letters? Your in-house writing? Are you gaining confidence that your writing is, in fact, good enough?

You have to believe in what you say in your writing. If you don't believe in what you are saying, there is no point in your writing it for others to read.

You have a story to tell, a legacy to share. You have a different perspective on a practice or process in your profession. You have ideas that will help others. You know from your own experiences in school that you can learn, and have learned, how to write. You know that with a bit of practice you can learn to write even better.

Most likely your writing is fine, especially when you choose your subject. When you do that, you will write with enthusiasm and competency. The really good news, however, is that you don't have just one chance to "get it right." You can write a second draft, a third draft, a fourth . . . as many drafts as you want.

Writers – all writers, but especially those who seek to be good – specialize in being "re-writers."

Share your writing stories with me. Tell me about the voices of encouragement and/or discouragement that you still hear. What impact do those voices have? E-mail the stories to: **stories@writechoiceservices.com**. In the subject line, type **good enough**.

Writers write to influence their readers, their preachers, their auditors, but always, at bottom, to be more themselves. ~ *Aldous Huxley*

Chapter 3

Seven Solid Benefits from Writing a Book

I was out of town providing logistics for a 10-day seminar when my first book officially became available to the public. When I had the opportunity, I went to Amazon.com and found my book listed there. Then I telephoned my wife.

"Go to Amazon.com and type my name in the search box," I said. I heard the clacking of a keyboard. I waited.

"Wow! That's so cool!" exclaimed Marta. My first published book was available on Amazon.com.

I called my sons, friends, relatives and colleagues and took them through the same drill. "Wow!" "Look at that!" "You did it." "I now know an author on Amazon.com."

I continued that series of phone calls with my next two books. I thoroughly enjoyed those calls, sharing my excitement with my family and friends and hearing the joy and excitement in their voices as well. You can experience similar moments when you hold your book in your hand.

Let's talk about the seven solid benefits to be gained from writing a book or articles or memoirs. Succinctly they are:

1) Authority
2) Marketing
3) Impact

4) Clarity
5) Creativity
6) Career
7) Legacy

Now let's look at each one in detail.

AUTHORITY

Throughout all of history, the general public has viewed authors of books as authorities in their field or on the topic about which they write. That image continues. The mere fact that an individual writes on a topic (article and/or book) and is published in some fashion (online, in a magazine, newspaper, industry publication, book) generates an image of being an authority on that topic. At the very least, one is viewed as having more knowledge and insight on the topic than those who have not been published.

A book is an impressive piece of work. A book communicates that the author has solid experience in a given area and/or has engaged in serious research. The author knows the topic more extensively, more fully than others in the field. A book conveys the idea that the author has something to share – information, insight, experience, opportunity – and articulates that information or insight very well.

When you write a book, you declare, "I've gained insight from my experiences and research and I've made some solid decisions that I want to share. I have a unique perspective on concepts and practices pertinent to my business, my industry, my process, which I believe can help you as well."

Writing a book is a great way to gain name recognition and to be sought out by others.

MARKETING

When an individual is published and subsequently is seen as an authority in the field, the individual has a new marketing moniker: authority, expert, published author. The public does take notice.

You probably have engaged in conversations in which other individuals in your industry have spoken of writing a book. But how many actually have followed through? Set yourself apart. Write the manuscript. Then publish it. Have your book in the marketplace. You now have an additional and very powerful marketing tool.

A book takes your thoughts, ideas, and insights (your authority) to places and venues that may not have been available to you or that you never considered, because there is only so much that one person can do to deliver a message. A book expands the capabilities and possibilities.

A well developed and well marketed book provides an ongoing revenue stream. The book serves as a foundation for generating other products, which in turn become new income streams.

Your book can serve as a very impressive business card. Imagine giving an autographed copy of your book to a potential client or to favored clients instead of the traditional business card.

When you write your manuscript and publish it as a book, you then create a website for the book and link it to your business website.

As you begin to write, you add to all of your bios – the standard press release biography, Facebook, LinkedIn, all the social media that you use – "author of the forthcoming book . . ." Of course, when the book is published, you go back to those sites and remove the word forthcoming so that the entry now reads: "author of the book . . ."

You are an author! You speak with authority in your field! You have a new arsenal for setting yourself and your business apart from the competition.

IMPACT

When an individual is published and recognized as an authority, is marketed, and the public takes notice, then the individual can have greater impact in the field, in the marketplace, in business. We may be talking a simple bump in the recognition meter but even a small bump is better than no bump. Moreover, the bumps and impact opportunities continue to build upon one another. Your influence grows. Your confidence increases.

Your book demonstrates your awareness of, and insights about, issues in that particular field. People view you as one who truly understands the area. Your reputation as expert grows.

Your thinking not only aligns with that of your readers but also articulates thoughts or concepts they wrestled with but could not express. Business opportunities increase as you are sought after because of your unique perspective or process.

CLARITY

To write effectively you have to have clarity. When you write on a topic in your industry/field/business/interests, you force yourself to gain that needed clarity of thought and expression. As you write articles or a book that is easily understood by the public, you demonstrate your keen ability to communicate even technical material with clarity.

Writing helps us to clear the clutter so that we focus upon basics, a core message. Once that core message emerges, then writing helps till the soil of our minds. That is where and when new ideas, new applications begin to grow. You are able to solve problems, address difficult issues, and even break down barriers. You become known as the one who can bring order amidst the possible chaos of the industry.

What if you simply want to write about family? The same concepts and impact apply. You bring a sense of order to what may be the disparate stories that circulate about Uncle Jerry, Aunt Sarah, Grandma Klingensmith, the black sheep brother, the daughter who moved away. You provide meaning for your family's existence and purpose.

And gaining strength in clarity will positively impact marketing ideas, because a new creativity emerges.

CREATIVITY

A side benefit of clarity is creativity. The clarity gained through writing clears cobwebs that cling to and hinder creativity. Achieving clarity sets free your imagination to envision new relationships, new solutions, and new ideas. Creativity surges as momentum builds and new possibilities come to mind.

A lot of what I have written above under clarity could be repeated here. Clarity enhances creativity. Creativity arises from focused, uncluttered thinking. Your confidence grows, so you look for opportunities to discover new products, new processes, new revenue streams or another book to write or articles to generate.

More writing? Absolutely! That is what all of these benefits of writing can do. I want to share an extended aside with you. As you continue to write, you may never really find it to be an easy adventure. The legendary sports writer, Red Smith, is attributed with voicing different variations of a common thought shared by writers: There is nothing to writing. All you do is sit down at a typewriter and open a vein.

I've been writing all of my life, and moments continue to arise in which Red Smith's observation seems very real. But I persevere because I know the joy of being published and in having people seek me out for advice on matters in the areas in which I have written a book or articles.

My younger son, Sean, was in high school when I began writing my books. Many times he sat at the computer doing his homework or playing a computer game while I sat at my desk writing. He would struggle with high school essays that required ten pages, typed, double-spaced, and he had a week or more to write it. I reminded him that ten pages is a standard day's output for me when I am writing. Sean just shook his head and muttered.

Recently Sean began studies for a master's degree in engineering. In the program so far he has had to write two, 25-page, typed, single-spaced papers. I mentioned to Sean that is the equivalent of 50 pages double-spaced or about one-third of a book.

That surprised him. Even though the professors determined the topic, Sean approached the writing with a different outlook. The act of writing remains a challenge, as it does for virtually everyone; however, Sean now senses some real joy in the process and in the finished product.

My older son, Joel, also took several graduate courses that required research papers. Joel honed a tremendous ability to write with clarity and confidence in the process. His research crystallized his thinking, which in turn gave him confidence about his perspective on the subject matter. Out of that confidence, Joel then wrote with amazing clarity.

CAREER

Imagine how nice "published author" or "recognized authority in the field" will look on your resume or in the company's annual report.

I'm not sure how many people express the desire to write a book but actually never do. In my research, I found one individual who put the number at eight out of ten. Then I found another article by the same individual who said nine out of ten. Another source mentioned 75 percent. The agreement seems to rest in the fact that many people express the desire but relatively few actually write a manuscript, much less take it to print to create a book.

Those who do develop a book concept, then write the manuscript and publish it, demonstrate highly prized personal traits: determination; ability to set, pursue and attain a goal; perseverance; critical thinking. Writing and publishing a book is a very impressive achievement.

Being able to list that achievement in your biography or resume can position you as a consultant or sought-after speaker.

My first book – *Healing Plants of the Bible: Then and Now* – came out in 2002. The book represents a merging of two areas of knowledge: scripture that I knew a lot about because of graduate study, and naturopathy/ alternative medicine that I had just begun to study and practice. The book was written for a particular niche of people. Over the years that niche continues to purchase the book but others outside of the niche have discovered it as well. I continue to receive inquiries from readers, herbalists and alternative health care practitioners about the contents of the book, about various alternative practices and my thoughts on these practices from a faith perspective.

Letters to My Sons: a Father's Faith Journey, my second book, I wrote in response to questions that my sons asked frequently. But my wider audience is people who hunger for an easily understood presentation of a moderate to liberal theology. The book encourages readers to have serious, heart-felt, down-in-the-dirt conversations with God. Subsequent to its publication, the book spawned keen interest from parents representing a wide range of theological perspectives. These parents simply wanted to read the faith journey of a father. Still others have found excitement in the book as an example for sharing a memoir.

Debbie Griffiths, R.N.C. and one of my writing clients, dreamed of writing a book that shared her life journey as encouragement for women who dream of being successful entrepreneurs. Debbie grew up "on the wrong side of the tracks." She describes herself in high school as wearing glasses with "Coke-bottle" lenses. Because of sensitive skin, she could never attain the golden glow that her classmates got from sun bathing. When she tried, she simply burned. Her fiancé was killed in an automobile accident caused by a drunk driver two weeks before their wedding. Debbie shares these stories and many more in her book, *Little Lady, Big Dream*, as she recounts her journey in overcoming persistent feelings of rejection and unworthiness and accompanying paralyzing fears to realize her dream of becoming an amazingly successful female entrepreneur and ultimately realizing her dream of building a multi-million dollar retirement community in her hometown.

<u>LEGACY</u>

In writing a book, you place your words and ideas in the public arena. If you are published in a magazine or journal or newspaper, there is a good chance that your article will be catalogued in some search engine somewhere. If your writing appears in a company publication, it will become part of the company archives. You will continue to have impact long after you have moved to another company or retired.

What you write can and will make a difference in the lives of those who read your writing. New relationships – professional and personal – will emerge. People will see you as a person of conviction who is willing to express his/her beliefs, perspectives, and understanding on issues or processes or products or . . . You fill in the blank.

If you write a family history or memoir, you help your extended family to understand better who the family is and what the family has stood for. You can shed new light on the "black sheep" or provide fascinating detail about a relative who always seemed to linger in the periphery but who actually had great impact within the lives of family members.

Please understand that the act of writing may never become an easy adventure. You may always feel very much akin to Red Smith's description of opening a vein. I still have those moments myself. But writing becomes an adventure upon which you are willing to embark.

Writers are people who make a difference in the world.

What difference do you hope your writing will make in your life? Would you take time to share those hopes with me? E-mail those thoughts to: **stories@writechoiceservices.com**. In the subject line type: **benefits**.

Writing, like life itself, is a voyage of discovery.
~ Henry Miller

Chapter 4

What I Know or What I Don't Know?

When I lead a writing seminar, I always ask this question: Should you write about what you know or about what you don't know? Seminar participants speak out, "What you know, of course. Why else would you write?" Others answer just as adamantly, "What you don't know because that forces you to do research. That way you will really know what you are saying." A rebuttal emerges from the "know group": Well, even if you know what you are writing about, you still do research to confirm your ideas and to expand what you know. From the "don't know group" comes this response: When you write about what you don't know and have to do research, then you don't come with any bias, predetermined notions or conclusions.

Both sides share similar arguments but from different starting points. Eventually some one asks me directly, "What is the answer?" With as serious an expression that I can muster, I say, "The answer is Yes." Silence settles upon the room. I smile; they laugh. Both approaches are possible.

Writing about what you know is the primary premise of this book. You have your own perspective on a business process. You have a different idea on the application of a theory. Your knowledge about your family provides insights that others do not have but hunger to hear. You have practical experiences, adventures, the stories handed down to you that inform who you are and what you do and why you do what you do. You share your unique perspective on the world. By writing these stories, you preserve and pass on that information not only to the current generation but also to the next generation and future generations as well.

What motivates people to write on a subject about which they know very little? Intellectual pursuit. Keen interest in a new area of knowledge or a new discipline. A desire to expand one's knowledge. Seeking out connections between what one knows and what one does not know.

We write about what we know because:

1) We have a good foundation: we have work experience, educational background and experience; practical knowledge;

2) We want to share insights we have gained;

3) We have developed a reputation for being good at or knowledgeable about something, and colleagues, peers and others seek us out;

4) We desire to strengthen our credibility based on our proven track record of success;

5) We believe ourselves to be an authority or want to be recognized as an authority in our field.

We write about what we don't know because:

1) Our interest in a particular subject motivates us to want to learn more and share that information;

2) We have developed a growing passion for a discipline, for family history, for memoir, or for streamlining a standard process, and writing helps us solidify our thinking;

3) We enjoy doing research, digging more deeply into a topic, putting form to that information and sharing it with others;

4) Someone challenges our thinking, our ideas or the process we use to do something, and that challenge triggers a need to engage in research and write up our findings.

The first time that I wrote about "what I don't know" had its beginning in the fall of 1977. I was part of a group of clergy in Lewiston-Auburn, Maine. Each fall we met to develop plans for various ecumenical services and celebrations for the coming program year. When discussion focused on Easter sunrise service, Art Kuehn, pastor of the American Baptist Church in Lewiston, announced, "Tim and I will plan that celebration and we will include clowns and balloons and a lot of good stuff."

I was a bit surprised, but I knew Art was a creative individual so I assumed he had a plan in mind. After the meeting I asked him what he knew about clowning.

"Not a thing," he answered. "How about you?"

"The same."

"Well, we've got a little more than six months to gather ideas and develop the celebration. We should be all right."

Art's confidence did little to ease my concern. We did have six months lead time, though!

At the time I was engaged in graduate studies. One of my courses was Aesthetics and Religious Education. Each class member chose a particular art form then developed and led a three-hour adventure in that medium. How to use the art form in worship or in education was the focus. One individual selected music. Another developed an experience with water color paints. Someone with an undergraduate degree in dance led us through different dances. Then, one student announced she would take us on a journey into clowning. Clowning! Yes!

After that clowning session, I dug deeper into the history of clowning. Were there clowns in the first century? What did they look like? What was a clown's official function? I wrote a sermon, "Jedidiah Becomes a Clown," for the Easter sunrise service 1978, which featured clowns and balloons and is still remembered some three decades later.

Fast forward about 18 months. I had moved to Peki, Volta Region, Ghana and was on staff at the Evangelical Presbyterian Seminary. From a United Methodist minister in the USA who had heard about my Jedidiah Becomes a Clown sermon and celebration came a letter. The pastor had a clown troupe in his church that provided clown ministry; however, the pastor had a problem. Some African-Americans who were a part of the clown ministry refused to wear the traditional white face of clowns. In his letter he asked, "Are there clowns among the Ghanaians and if so do they use some kind of clown make up?"

I lived in the bush. I did not have access to a library. All I could do was ask questions. And in asking questions, I quickly learned that clowns and clowning did not translate easily into the culture in which I lived. Then one day I attended a local harvest celebration. There was dancing and drumming and singing and chanting . . . and clowns! Or at least what I would describe as clowns. These people had orange and white markings all over their faces. I spoke with village elders, with the chief's linguist, and later with some of the people who had marked their faces. I learned the history and the significance of painting their faces white and orange. I wrote an article on all that I learned then mailed my article to the United Methodist minister back in the US. After reading about the Ghanaian people with white face and orange face, the reluctant clowns in the church group willingly put on white face.

A second adventure in writing about what I did not know came with my book *Healing Plants of the Bible: Then and Now*. When I entered religious bookstores in search of books on alternative medicine, I found such books shelved in the occult section. That bothered me. I was troubled by clergy who declared to their congregations that alternative medicine is either pagan or a tool of the devil. How did such thinking emerge?

I decided to research and find out. The impetus for my research came from my studies in naturopathy. Graduate work in seminary and practical experience as a minister had grounded me in scripture, theology and cosmology (the theological word for the study of the beginning of the universe). I had studied and even taught church history and historical theology – what ideas emerged over the centuries, what shaped the Church in particular and religion in general. The studies in naturopathy provided exposure to these "alternative" healing modalities.

I immersed myself in research on the origins of medicine, healing potions, health laws. I studied the connection, if any, in various ages and times between the Judaeo Christian tradition and healing and medicine. What impact did politics have on the growth of medical knowledge, understanding, practices and procedures?

My research led me to the Lloyd Library in Cincinnati, Ohio. The library maintains a collection of botanical, medical, pharmaceutical and scientific books and periodicals. When I entered the library, a research librarian asked me for a list of books, magazines and articles that I wanted. I gave her my list. She disappeared into the library stacks and several minutes later returned with a library cart filled with books, articles, reprints and documents far beyond what I had listed.

"They looked interesting and were near others that you had requested," she said. "Would you like me to search for more?"

Twice a day for three days the research librarian came to my study area with a new library cart filled with more resources. After three days, I realized that there would always be one more book, one more article, one more reference to hunt down and read. I had to stop at some point. When I found supporting information from three different sources for ideas and statements I wanted to make, I had reached my stopping point. Even with that limitation, I wound up with pages and pages and pages and pages of notes. The bibliography for *Healing Plants of the Bible* lists 124 sources.

In doing my research, I discovered that the practice of calling alternative medicine pagan arose from the simple fact that the founders or developers of such practices were pagans in their beliefs. Yet, Hippocrates was a pagan but is known and accepted as the father of modern medicine. Euclid was a pagan. Euclid is called the father of geometry. We accept Euclid's mathematical discoveries and we certainly use "modern medicine." The label of "tool of the devil" emerged in part from the turmoil within the Church during the Reformation. Common women who were knowledgeable about plants and herbs provided better remedies and healing than the formally trained doctors. The need to maintain male dominance in medicine, protect the merchants in the marketplace, and political/religious intrigue fueled the ideas of alternative medicine being pagan or a tool of the devil.

Letters to My Sons: a Father's Faith Journey was totally based upon what I knew. The chapters took the form of letters to my sons. Whatever I shared with Joel and Sean would have to be based on what I knew from my studies, work and parenting. I would not consult any textbooks or classroom notes.

This book began as simply sharing what I know about writing from all the writing I have done throughout my career, and especially since focusing completely on being a writer and writing coach. I've engaged in research over the years and have made pages and pages of notes and quotes when reading books and articles on writing. I've reviewed those notes . . . and obviously used some of the quotes.

When you think about what you know, go beyond traditional learning, book learning, school and education. Consider all the knowledge that you have gained from life experiences – the "school of hard knocks" – or from being a part of a family. What about all of the after school jobs and summer jobs and part-time jobs and full-time jobs you have had? What did you learn from those? What have you learned as you have worked with people from different backgrounds or who hold different values?

What you know is more than simple facts. You have your memories and your interpretation of events which could very well differ from your sibling's memory and interpretation of the same event.

What do you remember of your grade school teachers and classmates? I went to half-day kindergarten. Our class met on the stage in the school gym. Our teacher was diagnosed with cancer and we had a substitute teacher for most of the year. In first grade, I was diagnosed with an ulcer. My mom was embarrassed. How could her six-year-old son have an ulcer? What I remember is the horrendous pain I was in and the ugly, foul tasting, pale pea-green medicine I had to take and the doctor being patient and gentle with me. He apologized for having to prescribe such ugly medicine but he wanted me to get better, to get over the pain. I took the medicine. Throughout my life, whenever I see that shade of green, my stomach still does a bit of a flip, while my emotions recall the compassion of the doctor.

The smell of wood fires reminds me of my family gathered in the family room at Thanksgiving or Christmas and a wonderful fire burning in the fireplace. I also recall going to saw mills as a lad with my dad. He owned the saw mills and at each sawmill there was a smoldering, burn pile. Often we would run into my grandfather at one of the saw mills as he operated the huge skidder. This is some of what I know and can write about.

When the fragrance of coconut oil wafts through the air, my guess is most people think of the beach, suntan lotion, and relaxation. I used to have those thoughts. Then I lived in Ghana for three years and coconut oil was one of several cooking oils. Now when I encounter the fragrance of coconut oil, I remember Peki, the village in which I lived.

You have oceans of information amassed from sounds, tastes, odors. This is part of what you know. You know maxims and parables and proverbs that ring true in your life. You have an understanding of first causes, politics, faith, love, the world, other nations, and . . . all of that is a part of what you know. And that is what you are going to write about.

In *On Writing: a Memoir of the Craft*, Stephen King comments: "I think you begin by interpreting 'write what you know' as broadly and inclusively as possible . . . Write what you like, then imbue it with life and make it unique by blending in your own personal knowledge of life, friendship, relationships, sex and work."

Do you write about what you know or about what you don't know? The answer is unequivocally, Yes! And you write with passion and intent. Ultimately, writing is about all that you know and have experienced and will experience and want to know. You write with confidence about the truth that you know: about your work, your family, your adventures, your profession, your hobby, your faith . . . your view of the world and from the research that you do.

Which do you prefer to write – what you know or what you don't know? Perhaps you take both approaches depending upon the topic and your interest. Tell me how you make your decision. E-mail me with your thoughts: **stories@writechoiceservices.com**. Put **KDK** in the subject line.

It is easy to lose sight of the fact that writers do not write to impart knowledge to others; rather they write to inform themselves. ~Judith Guest

Chapter 5

Using Journals & Accumulated Notes for Writing

The above comment from novelist Judith Guest appears in the foreword she wrote for Natalie Goldberg's book *Writing Down the Bones*. The words grabbed my attention the first time I read them. I thought writers did just the opposite – writers write to impart knowledge to others because writers are informed. The more immersed I became in my own writing the more I experienced the truth of Guest's words. In writing, we inform ourselves. Putting words on paper forces us to wrestle with what we believe. Do I want to put this in writing? Do I believe what I am saying? We soon realize what we know as well as what we don't know. Once informed, then we decide how and what to share with the world. Chapter 4 reminds us of that.

This truth came to life for me when I wrote *Letters to My Sons*. My journals played a critical part in that adventure. When I began writing to Joel and Sean, I had a long list of topics; too many topics I soon realized. What I had before me was the start of a theological treatise. That was not what my sons wanted. Sean and Joel simply sought the basics of my journey, not all the nuances of my faith and theology. I put aside the seminary textbooks from my graduate studies, the notebooks filled with notes from lectures I had heard and the papers I had written over the years. I turned to my journals for clarity. I read my reflections on various events, classes that I had taken in college and graduate school, comments on family members and other individuals. What did I remember about those events or classes? What were situations that I saw as unique and what did I learn from them? What books, scripture, prayers did I mention frequently? What issues did I wrestle with? How did I describe the impact of all of that on my faith or on my personal journey or both?

My journals were invaluable in helping me sort out what I believed. In the writing of *Letters*, I came to understand Guest's comment. I had begun the process thinking that I was sharing with Joel and Sean what I knew. I discovered along the way that in writing for them I came to understand and solidify my beliefs. I learned how they took shape. I found my truth.

I imagine that you, the readers of this book, have an accumulation of journals or diaries or file folders filled with notes, stories, comments on events, reflections. When you look at your writing, as you leaf through the pages, you tell yourself, "There must be a book in here somewhere. Maybe even two or three." Perhaps you allow yourself to dream big and declare, "I know I've got a best seller hiding in these notes."

Journals and diaries – real ones, the nonfiction variety – have become best sellers, even classics. You know them as *The Diary of Anne Frank* and Henry David Thoreau's *Walden: Life in the Woods*. Some lesser known journals that have had large readership are: *The Freedom Writers Diary* by the Long Beach, California High School students who became known as the Freedom Writers along with their teacher, Erin Gruwell, and *Leaves from the Notebook of a Tamed Critic*, Reinhold Niebuhr's reflections from 13 years as a parish minister.

Journals and diaries are the format for many works of fiction as well: Susan Kaufman's *Diary of a Mad Housewife* and Jeff Owens' *Diary of a Wimpy Kid* series are two of the best known ones. Amazon.com lists over 295,000 entries relevant to diary while the word "journal" triggers 946,000 entries and "memoirs" sports 315,000 references.

There is a proven history that books generated from diaries and journals can become best-selling books. I am not suggesting that you want to take your journal or your diary or your pile of random notes and write the next New York Times best-selling Diary of . . . or Reflections from . . . What I am suggesting is that you turn to your journals, diaries and notes for ideas for writing. You just might find the beginning of a book or the foundation for a book (or books) in what you have written in your journals or diaries. The emphasis is upon finding a beginning or foundation for a theme, not a complete book hidden within the entries.

In my study, I have a stack of journals. At least 15 of the journals are filled with writing on every page. I have another five journals "in process" that I use, or have used, to record different adventures in my life. In my supply closet, six "empty" journals of various sizes and bindings await their turn. I do leaf through the pages of my journals from time to time. I don't need a specific reason. I enter the pages as if on a treasure hunt. What gem might I find in the pages this time? Will those gems then trigger new writing ideas? Sometimes the answer is yes. Most of the time, the journey through the pages triggers additional thoughts and reflections, which in turn generate new journal entries. I am shaping what I see, believe, and understand.

My most detailed and complete journal is a record of my work with the Evangelical Presbyterian Church in Ghana. From July 1978 through October 1981, I worked as an education specialist for the Church and as principal of its seminary. With rare exception, I wrote in my journal each day. As I look back on those entries, I realize that what I have is more of a diary than a journal. (In a diary, you record events of the day, things that happened. In a journal, you may or may not record events of the day but you take time to reflect on those events or you simply focus on some thought or incident and "journal" about it.) But those entries along with all of the letters I wrote to my parents, which they saved, and the newsletter articles that I wrote monthly record the amazing history of those three years of my life.

When I went to Ghana with my journal, I had a secret hope that whatever I wrote in those blank pages could become a very marketable book. Thirty years later, I have yet to write that book and I know that I will never write the book that I thought I would write – the adventures of living in a bush village, travelling around a developing nation on dirt roads, grass roads and no roads, occasionally having the experience of being the first white person some children had ever seen. However, reflections from that journal have become illustrations for essays and stories I have written. They helped me recognize some common themes that continued in my life even though I've lived in vastly different settings and conditions.

Through my own reading, writing and research, I have learned that journals and diaries "cleaned up and edited" do not necessarily make a good manuscript. Even if the contents of the journal are realigned or reconfigured, they still would not make a good manuscript. What journals and diaries and notes do offer is the basis of a story of *you* that you might want to tell. Cox and Kooser in *Writing Brave and Free* talk about approaching a story "sideways or tangentially." The story is found within the pages of the journal, the pages of your reflections. You begin to see a common thread or a pattern or an idea emerge and you write about it.

Our journals represent our growth journeys. How we handled difficult situations. The moments in our lives in which we stumbled. The barriers we conquered. Accomplishments we achieved. Events we celebrated. Successes we enjoyed. Your journal may be a record of how you came to think differently about an idea or a process, a situation or belief. Those entries, sorted, compiled and expounded upon might become an amazing book for others to read. If you take the plunge and write that manuscript, you will have experienced for yourself the truth of Guest's words. You have written not so much to impart knowledge to others as you have written to inform yourself, to clarify your thinking. The bonus is that others will want to read what you have written and benefit from your words.

I discovered as I did the research for my book, *Healing Plants of the Bible*, that I had had a life-long interest in healing, especially from a non-traditional perspective. Grandma Morrison found comfort and strength in the work and ministry of Kathryn Kuhlman. She watched Kuhlman's television specials, read her books, supported her ministry, and sent names of family members to the ministry for prayer. Grandma shared stories about the healings that Kathryn Kuhlman worked. The stories fascinated me. The healing stories in scripture fascinated me when I was a child and still do now that I am an adult. The stories trigger lots of questions in my mind: what did the healer feel; what did the person who was healed feel; what did the crowds see or sense or think. In one of the ministry settings in which I was an associate pastor, the senior pastor opened the church to host a weekend healing conference and, much to my chagrin, involved us in the actual healing service. As the service began, I had two fears: What if my prayers for healing didn't work? And, what if they did? I wasn't sure which concerned me more. While living in Ghana, frequently the only remedies available for treating anything were homemade remedies, the concoctions that local herbalists prepared. When I returned to the United States and to traditional ministry, I always engaged in continuing education opportunities and I looked for seminars and courses on healing.

What I thought had been a relatively recent surge of interest in non-traditional methods of healing because of my three years in Ghana, was actually another segment of my life-long fascination with healing and wholeness. That discovery emerged when I read through the journal entries I had written over several decades. Seeing that thread in my life as recorded in my journals provided additional determination to write my book.

My colleague and mentor, the late Dr. Patricia Allen Brown, and I often discussed journaling. She reminded me that if I discovered when I skimmed through my journal entries that I wrote repeatedly about some things, even though months or years separated those similar entries, I needed to look at those writings. What was I trying to tell myself? What lesson was I struggling to learn? What challenge was I sidestepping? Approach your journals, diaries or notes with a similar view and you may discover fertile ground for writing.

We write to inform ourselves? Yes, we write to inform ourselves, to gain clarity in our thinking and ideas. Such writing becomes the foundation for what we tell others. In our journals, diaries and random notes, we have allowed ourselves truly to ponder our thoughts, to wrestle with troubling issues, or to reflect on emerging insights. We have written and re-written them until we are comfortable with what they say. It makes sense to us out of our experiences. Now we share those thoughts and that knowledge with others.

This is not necessarily an easy process, though. I am never certain what emotions or thoughts or reactions will emerge as I sift through the pages of my journals. I have discovered occasionally that what once had been "truth" in my life, according to words that I wrote, has taken on a new form while other "truths" have become more solidly framed. Always there are other journal entries which are best described as thoughts in process – issues and ideas that I continue to reflect upon.

Good writing is about telling the truth, specifically our personal truth or as Chapter Four discussed: What we know and don't know. As writers, we have a particular passion to understand who we are.

Give yourself permission to wander through your journals, your diaries or whatever pile of notes you may have generated. Look for recurring themes. Listen to your voice speak to you anew. What insights do you discern? What sparks your imagination?

You may discover a lot of potential writing ideas. List them all. Make notes on how to find those journal entries again so that you can re-read them should you choose to write more fully on the idea. And celebrate the richness of the material that you uncover.

The next chapter will help you determine which of these possible topics should be your focus.

The rhythm of walking generates a kind of rhythm of thinking, and the passage through a landscape echoes or stimulates the passage through a series of thoughts.
~ Rebecca Solnit from her book *Wanderlust: A History of Walking*

Have you walked a labyrinth yet? Or used one of the labyrinths printed in the appendix? If not, I encourage you to take time now to experience either of the two labyrinths.

*In all my writing I tell the story of my life,
over and over again.* ~ Isaac Bashevis Singer

Chapter 6

The Secret to Finding Your Book Topic

Take time to find the story. William Zinsser gives that advice to the adults who participate in his "People and Places" writing class. One student from the "People and Places" class decided to write about a fire that had burned the church she attended. She shared with the class that she could interview the pastor or the church musician or one of the firefighters or some other church employee or member. Zinsser challenged her to go deeper. Specifically he said, "When you go to church in the next few weeks just sit there and think about the fire. After three or four Sundays the church is going to tell you what that fire means. God is going to tell that church to tell you what the fire means." (Zinsser, *On Writing Well*, pps. 253 – 257)

Curiously, no writing ever occurs in the "People and Places" class. Zinsser does tell his students that he will gladly accept any story or writing each student wishes to submit to him once the course is completed, but the focus in this particular writing course is *preparing* to write: finding the real story that will speak to the reader.

Take time to find the story. I tell that to my writing clients. Take time to find the story. I tell that to myself. Even if numerous ideas come to mind as writing possibilities, take time to discern which is best. Which idea tugs at your heart and stirs your soul? Identify it. Embrace it. Write about it.

To be an effective writer, you need to wait patiently. Listen to your heart. Connect deeply with your soul.

This chapter reveals the process that I personally use and have my clients use to find the perfect book topic or article topic, particularly when several ideas fight for attention. The process has had a proven history of success for nearly 800 years. However, when it began, the process had nothing to do with writing and everything to do with understanding sacred texts.

On a Friday morning in the fall of 1975, I sat in my study and stared at the wastebasket. I had just tossed another balled up sheet of paper into the basket. That paper wad joined myriad others that I had tossed in throughout the week. Each crumpled sheet of paper represented a false start on my sermon. Sunday loomed especially large.

I had never experienced writer's block as severe as this. I had completed the study and research that I always did. I had several pages of notes but each time I began to write, I became stuck. With the hope that some clarity would surface, I read one of the scripture lessons again. I read the passage slowly. I re-read it. I focused upon each word. I heard a voice speak. That voice reflected on the situation in the scripture, added other insights, offered comments about the crowd. I wrote down all that I heard. It made sense. I had a sermon! I had let go of logic and had journeyed deep inside myself.

Over the years, whenever I smacked up against writer's block, I repeated this process: read, read again, wait, and listen. Each time I eventually gained clarity and direction. After nearly two decades of engaging in this process, I learned that it had a name - *lectio divina* – and that the process had been around for nearly eight centuries.

Lectio divina, which is Latin, translates literally as "divine reading" or "sacred reading" and was a mainstay in monasteries and among clergy for centuries. Many centuries ago when monks found themselves stymied by scripture, they had no commentaries to consult, no concordances, no chain reference Bibles, and, of course, no internet search engines! All they had were their Bibles and God.

When a monk encountered a difficult text or obscure passage, all he could do was "sit with it" – read the difficult passage over and over and over again. He would ponder the passage, even pray over it. Through this process, the monk hoped to puzzle out or discern the meaning of the passage. This process became known as *lectio divina*.

Over the centuries, lectio divina has taken shape as a Four-Step Process: *lectio, meditatio, oratio, and contemplatio.*

The Four Steps of *Lectio Divina*

Lectio:

The simple translation is "read." In *lectio* we read a portion of writing. We may read it several times. We may even elect to read aloud. We read until a particular word or phrase takes hold in our mind.

Meditatio:

We reflect. We enter into the word or the phrase that has taken hold of us and we reflect upon it.

Oratio:

"Respond" is the primary thought. We respond in some fashion to the word or phrase that has taken hold of us and has been the focus of our meditation.

Contemplatio:

Think simply of "rest." After reading, reflecting and responding, we "rest" in the word. We sit in God's presence, open and ready to receive whatever God sends.

The challenge of *lectio divina* is the need for us to relinquish or suspend our preconceived notions and defenses about what we are reading so that we might really hear what God says to us from within.

I use *lectio divina* with my own writing to bring focus to an elusive theme. I have led writing clients through the four steps as well to assist them in finding clarity and focus in their writing.

How do we apply this to a discernment process connected with a writing project?

You apply *lectio divina* to a collection of your own writing, journaling or notes that you have made as you have thought about a writing project. You may have a list of ideas that you keep in a notebook. You might want to leaf through your journals and jot down recurring themes or ideas that jump out at you. Do ideas, themes, or topics run through your mind? Write those down. The key is to create a list of potential topics or ideas. You will then use that list for your *lectio divina* process.

The Process of Discernment for Writing

Lectio - READ

Take your list and read through it. If you wish, you can simply read through a segment of a journal if it contains material you believe you want to expand into a book. Regardless of whether you choose to read or to skim the material, do so several times. You may want to read aloud. Continue reading until a particular word or phrase takes hold in your mind. This word or phrase may actually occur in the material you are reading or it may be something that enters your mind because of what you are reading. Write it down – the word or the phrase or the concept.

Meditatio - REFLECT

Now reflect upon the word, the phrase or concept that you identified in the lectio process. "Chew" on it for awhile. "Look" at it from different sides or angles. What does the word, the phrase, the concept offer? How does it speak to you? Why does it speak to you? What do you sense that it calls you to say or to do? Make notes of all that comes to your mind. Do not reject any thought or any concept simply because it seems weird or strange or even because you do not understand it. We are still in the process of discernment so write down everything that comes to mind.

Oratio - RESPOND

You now have a choice at this point but the end result will be the same.

If you know yourself to be a spiritual or religious person and if you are comfortable with a more traditional concept of prayer, then proceed to option A below.

If you describe yourself as more spiritual than religious or if traditional prayer is not a part of your make up, I recommend you follow option B.

If neither A nor B speaks to you, then focus on option C.

OPTION A: Now is the time to engage in prayer as you understand it. Remembering that *oratio* means "respond," offer thanksgiving for the emerging insights that have come to you. Or acknowledge that you remain in a muddled state and ask for greater clarity. Still give thanks for the steps toward clarity that have emerged. Speak however you feel led: with words, without words, with gestures only, with the quiet yearning of your heart. The key is to respond.

OPTION B: For those who resonate more with being spiritual than religious: Offer to the Universe or Spirit your energy of gratitude for what has been made known to you so far. If cloudiness still prevails, then ask for greater clarity from Spirit/Universe. Wait patiently. Focus on the inner yearnings of your heart, mind and soul. Acknowledge the emotions that you find therein. Express gratitude for the awakening that is unfolding.

OPTION C: Assume an attitude or posture of gratitude and receptivity. Express that gratitude in a manner that feels appropriate. Take note of any possible yearnings that might be present in your heart, mind and soul. Express those yearnings. Then return to your attitude or posture of gratitude.

Contemplatio - REST

OPTION A – sit in silence in the presence of God while remaining open and ready to receive whatever God offers to you.

OPTION B – sit in silence in the presence of the Universe/Spirit while remaining open and ready to receive whatever the Universe/Spirit offers to you.

OPTION C – sit in silence, "simply being" while remaining open and ready to receive whatever your inner yearnings bring to your attention.

ALL OPTIONS: Throughout this process, it is critical that you let go of images of what you want to hear or hope to hear. Instead, focus upon remaining open and receptive. Then simply receive. Listen closely. Listen keenly. Listen clearly. And receive. If you can make notes without disturbing the flow of creative energy and emerging thoughts, do so. Otherwise, simply remain open to receiving and when the flow of information ceases, write furiously to capture as much as you can.

Ideally, a concept has emerged and grabbed your attention. Through this process you have discerned your writing project theme. This is your book topic.

What if, instead of identifying a single topic, the *lectio divina* process has only reduced the number of possibilities? Do not despair. You have achieved some clarity even though a bit of fog still lingers. Maybe through the process you have identified several (three, four, five, or more) viable ideas. Wait a day or two or even three and work through the lectio divina process again. This time focus on the ideas that surfaced from your initial *lectio divina* experience.

Keep using *lectio divina* until you attain clarity. Maybe you only wait a couple of hours before engaging in the process again. Or you choose to wait a day or two. You decide. You use the smaller list; the one generated from your last lectio divina adventure. Each time you engage in the lectio divina, greater clarity should emerge. Keep at the process until you have that one theme that you absolutely know is The Theme and it came to you not through intellectual gymnastics but from a truly spiritual process in which you have gone outside of your intellect and into your heart and soul.

Trust the process. Pay attention to what speaks to you from your heart and your soul.

Don't discard all the other concepts or themes that appeared in the initial *lectio divina* process but were eliminated the next time you used lectio divina. As you write your book based upon your newly identified theme, you may discover that some of the other ideas will become sub themes in your book. Another possibility is that they become future writing projects.

Most of my clients come to me with several ideas for books. They are not sure which topic is the right topic or the best topic for them to focus on. I tell them about lectio divina and give them guidelines on using *lectio divina*. Every time, each client has gained the clarity he/she needed. Several continue to use *lectio divina* each time they begin a writing project. In doing this, they know they will write on the topic that speaks to their heart and mind.

If you have questions about the process, contact me at:
tim@writechoiceservices.com.
Put **lectio divina** in the subject line.

True originality consists not in a new manner but in a new vision. ~ *Edith Wharton*

Chapter 7

Mind Mapping Your Book

If you have followed the *lectio divina* process outlined in chapter 6, you now have a book topic. The time has come to begin writing or at least to generate some kind of outline or map to guide your writing. That is the primary focus of this chapter.

Perhaps when you engaged in the *lectio divina* process, you ended with two or three possible topics instead of just one. Or maybe *lectio divina* simply did not work for you. The latter part of this chapter will discuss what to do if that is your situation.

An outline of some fashion is what many writers have used over the years to guide them in writing a book. Actually, the traditional outline format has been around for centuries. Research has not been able to identify who created the first recognizable outline; however, history does indicate that ancient Roman and Greek rhetoricians suggested having specific sections to one's presentation. And Cicero as early as 46 BCE recommended having a section in one's presentation called *partitio* that indicated what would follow. We learned in grade school how to create an outline to help us in our writing assignments or to generate a report or term paper. Some folks continue to use the traditional outline model.

I use a variation of the traditional outline when I write. I don't use Roman numerals and letters, then numbers, then small roman numerals, and so forth. I merely indent when I think I've shifted my thought or information. I use a lot of arrows as well to indicate that I want to move this paragraph to here and that one there.

Another approach to creating an outline for a book is to brainstorm the number of chapters you believe your book will have. Next, you consider how many points you want to make in each chapter and how many pages you want to have in your book. Divide the number of pages you want in your book by the number of points you plan to address. That resulting number represents the standard number of pages you will need to devote to each point in order to attain the size of book you desire.

Each of these processes works; however, each involves linear thinking and many folks today have moved beyond linear thinking. That is where mind mapping your book enters in. My clients who have tried mind mapping have had tremendous success with the process. Some have even spoken of a rush of creativity emerging as they generated their "map."

Tony Buzan receives credit for developing and popularizing mind mapping in the 1970s. Over the years, variations have appeared. Those variations often address a particular discipline or group of individuals.

In mind mapping, one writes down a central idea and then brainstorms new and related ideas that radiate from the central idea. Mind mapping is two-dimensional, as opposed to the linear process of traditional outlining. Originally, mind mapping was taught as a means to encourage creative problem solving. In our situation, the problem to be solved is creating chapter titles, chapter content, and a general flow of materials. Mind mapping provides individuals with an amazing perspective of the inter-relatedness of ideas, concepts or themes.

What follows is a basic mind mapping process for general use in problem solving. After this section, I will show you how to use mind mapping to write your book.

Necessary tools:

1) Paper – large paper; at least 11 x 14 inches; 14 $1/2$ x 17 inches or a newsprint pad provide more room;

2) Pencils, pens, crayons or markers in a variety of colors.

Strongly recommended:

1) Print all of your words instead of writing them so that what you put on your mind map is easily read, especially when information begins to get a bit crowded;

2) Use very simple phrases and, if possible, just single words;

3) Be ready to engage in serious brainstorming;

4) Position your paper in the "landscape" mode.

The Process:

1) In the center of your paper, print your core idea or theme and draw a circle around it;

2) Radiating from the core idea like spokes on a wheel, write sub-themes for the central theme; circle each of those sub-themes individually, and connect each one by a line to the central theme;

3) Using a different color of marker/pen/pencil, continue brainstorming by listing ideas that branch off from those sub-themes as you did in (2) above; circle each of these and draw a line connecting that word or very simple phrase to the sub-theme word. There may be even smaller branches coming off those branches. If they come to mind, put them in;

4) Remember always to use lines to connect each smaller theme or topic back to the relevant larger theme;

5) By following the lines, you should return to the core idea relatively easily;

6) Study, burrow into, reflect on what you have mapped as you move along;

7) As you review your mind map, you may want to add even smaller branches . . . or you may want to remove some of the branches, or combine some of them;

8) Set aside your completed mind map and return to it later when you can look at it with fresh eyes;

9) Review what you have mapped out. Does it still make sense to you? Does it need any tweaking?

Use these nine steps as the foundation for generating a mind map to help you gain greater focus for any project: planning a party, getting a new product ready for market, etc. Then the following five steps are specifically for writing. These steps represent a compilation from various sources, and they explain how I use mind mapping. *(A sample mind map can be found on page 75 in the appendix.)*

- **STEP 1:** Write your core idea or theme in the center of a huge piece of paper. Circle that word so that it does not get "lost" in the rest of the process.

- **STEP 2:** Brainstorm! Engage in serious brainstorming. Print all the words or concepts that relate to your core idea or theme. Draw a circle or box around each one that you write so that you remember/recognize it as a single idea. Words can get a little crowded as this process unfolds.

- **STEP 3:** When you believe that you have finished with your brainstorming, study all the words and ideas that surround your core idea. Identify the words that "jump out" at you as main ideas that logically generate from the core idea. Use a colored pencil/marker to draw a line from each of these main ideas to the core idea. In doing this you have most likely identified your chapter themes.

- **STEP 4:** Now look at the remaining words. Under which chapter do you see these words appearing? Using a different color for each chapter that you have identified, draw a line from each of the remaining words to the chapter word that relates to it. When you finish with the lines, your mind map could look like a mosaic.

- **STEP 5:** In this step, you refine your document and create an easy-to-read mind map. Take another sheet of paper. Put your core word/theme in the center again. Now look at the words you have designated as "chapter words." With the understanding that nothing is set in stone in this process, place the chapter words around your theme word. Mark with appropriate designation the chapter words in the order you think they may occur, i.e., Chapter 1, Chapter 2, Chapter 3, etc. Draw the connecting line from each chapter word to the core idea. You've probably already guessed what you do next: all of the words that you have connected to the chapter word during the brainstorming process you now place around the specific chapter word. Of course, you circle each of these words and draw a line from that circled word to the chapter word. When you finish, you now have a mind map that is clear and easy to read.

What if you are still struggling to settle on one specific book topic? You have worked with lectio divina and you either couldn't get the process to work for you or you narrowed the topics down to two or three. Turn to mind mapping to gain clarity.

Engage in the mind mapping process for each possible book theme or topic that you have. Follow all of the steps precisely as outlined. That means you begin with a large sheet of paper, placed in the landscape position. In the center of that paper, you write down your topic, circle that word and proceed to the next step. Work each stage to the extent that you can. If you feel blocked in the process such that you can't flesh out words and branches, stop. Put that mind map to the side and begin with your next topic. Go as deeply into the mind mapping process as you can. Continue with creating a mind map for each topic/theme.

When you have finished with each of the mind maps that you need to create, line them up and study them. Which mind map is the most extensive? Which mind map was easiest to generate? Which sparked the most energy within you as you created it? Which makes the most sense? Ideally, the same mind map will emerge as the answer to all four questions. That is your book topic.

Now study the mind map for your specific book topic. Look for possible inter-connecting themes between chapter words and their sub words. Do you address a topic in more than one chapter? If so, how will those treatments differ? Or do you see that the topic would be better handled in just one chapter? Do any sub-themes begin to emerge that might merit treatment as a chapter? Earlier, you had given an order to the chapters. Does your more thorough look at these chapters suggest a need to re-order or re-position some of them? As you begin to write, and throughout your writing, continue to review your map. You may discern myriad other ideas, words, topics, themes to consider, or you may want to delete some. The mind map lends itself to that creative reflective process.

Books and articles abound on virtually every aspect of writing. There is a lot of sage advice available. Read what makes sense to you, but know you have to stop reading and start writing sometime. As you read, decide what makes sense to you, what you believe will work for you. Go with that material.

Some readers are more computer oriented in all that they do so using pencil and paper to mind map is not appealing. There are various mind mapping software programs available. I encourage you to use your search engine to identify some of them. Several companies offer free downloads of basic mind mapping programs. These basic programs are often sufficient

for writing purposes; of course, as with any free downloads, you can purchase upgrades. I use a program from TheBrain.
http://www.thebrain.com/purchase?aid=1224

I am interested in hearing how you have used mind mapping (whether by pencil and paper or by software program) in your writing journey.
E-mail those stories to:
stories@writechoiceservices.com.
In the subject line, insert **Mind mapping**.

The difference between the right word and the almost right word is the difference between lightening and the lightening bug. ~ *Mark Twain*

Chapter 8

Sharpening Your Focus

Let's review what we have considered so far. We discussed the red ink syndrome and other factors that keep us from writing. We looked at some of the benefits that can be accrued by writing and publishing a book. We considered the advantages of writing about things you know and the advantages of writing about things that you don't know but elect to research. We journeyed through journals and notes and scraps of paper in search of potential writing themes. Then came the discussion on *lectio divina* to help us identify the right book topic for this particular moment. And we just finished our discussion of mind mapping, which helps us generate a rough outline for our book. Or, if *lectio divina* did not bring the clarity that was needed for a book topic, I showed you how to use mind mapping to identify a topic. Surely the time for beginning to write our manuscript has arrived!

Not quite. When I work with my clients, I challenge them to complete a few more steps that provide an invaluable foundation as they write the initial draft of their manuscript. I encourage you to do the same. These steps come from some of the components that are part of a query letter.

If you are writing with the intention of being published, then you need to familiarize yourself with the query letter and its contents. A query letter is the document that you send alone or with segments of your manuscript to an agent with the intent of getting the agent to agree to present your manuscript to publishers for consideration. Some small to mid-size publishers welcome un-agented submissions, which means you can submit your query letter directly to the submissions editor or acquisition editor for consideration. The contents of a query letter are rather standard. The descriptions of the items requested may vary a bit from publisher to publisher or agent to agent, but the concepts remain essentially the same.

Here is a list of materials or information that is most frequently called for in a query letter or submission packet:

1) Working title of the manuscript;

2) A 150-word synopsis of the manuscript;

3) The table of contents;

4) The number of pages in the manuscript;

5) The number of words in the manuscript;

6) Projected completion date for the manuscript (if it is not yet finished);

7) The basis of your authority to write this manuscript – personal experience, extensive research, work experience, education, etc.;

8) Detailed description of the audience (to whom, for whom is the manuscript written);

9) Brief description of your marketing plan – what you, the author, will do to market the manuscript when it is published and has become a book;

10) Your platform – what schools claim you as an alumni; to what service organizations do you belong; are you a member of a faith community; do you hold membership in any trade or professional organizations; do you have some kind of following as a speaker, industry guru, etc.;

11) Summary of the competition – what other books are on the market that are similar in nature to your projected book;

12) Analysis of your manuscript as it differs from the competition – what new information, new perspective, new insight does your manuscript provide;

13) Submit two or three of your best sample chapters – not necessarily the first three nor any three consecutive chapters.

Before giving my clients the green light to begin writing, I ask them to provide me with a table of contents, a 150-word synopsis of their manuscript and a detailed description of their intended audience – to whom are they writing. Notice I do not ask for a title. Most clients already have a title in mind. I suggest that they view their title as a working title and to keep themselves open to changing that working title as the manuscript takes shape. I encourage you to do the same. Complete your manuscript. Then determine your title.

The synopsis describes what the book is about. The back-cover copy of virtually every soft-cover book includes a synopsis of that particular book, containing about 150 words. If a book is hardcover, then the synopsis is found on the fly leaf of the dust jacket, and may contain a few more words. The synopsis serves a twofold purpose: 1) it provides a clear and enticing description of the book's content and 2) it motivates the individual to check out the table of contents, browse through some pages and buy the book. The synopsis needs to be clear, concise, and attention-grabbing.

I explain to my clients that seasoned writers generally craft the synopsis after they have finished writing their manuscripts, because then they know exactly what is contained within the book. I encourage beginning or emerging writers to write the synopsis first so that you know where your path is leading. The synopsis serves as a measure for all that is written in the manuscript. As you write, ask yourself: Am I on track with my writing, with my contents? Am I keeping to my intended theme?

Don't begin your synopsis with "This book is about." A synopsis that begins with those four words will invariably be weak or lack precision. Jump right into the description. Janet Litherland begins the synopsis to *Song of the Heart* with "What would it be like to reconnect with a high-school sweetheart after more than two decades?" The synopsis for my first book opens: "Combining history, anecdotal history, legends and traditions, *Healing Plants of the Bible: Then and Now* provides an informative look at faith concerns and healing practices and suggests that the two have been intertwined since creation itself."

Grab some soft-cover books from your own bookshelves. Look at the back cover. Read the synopses that you find. Or go into a bookstore and find the section for the genre in which you plan to write. Check out the synopses for the books you find. Search any of the online bookstores. Call up a particular book and read the synopsis. It is there as part of the information about the book. Get a feel for how synopses are worded. You will be able to revise your synopsis as you go along so don't be concerned with getting it "tight" from the beginning. However, be as clear and specific as you can.

If you are writing a memoir, your synopsis should describe the years, events, or individuals upon which you will focus: my high school years; coming of age during the Viet Nam War; encounters with Uncle Walt; what most of my family didn't know about. If your book topic deals with a new approach you have developed in your profession, your synopsis may include something like this: a more efficient way to product delivery by tweaking the initial stage of production; re-arranging steps 1 – 2 and 3 to 3 – 1 and 2 to cut costs and expedite delivery; a proven way to approach a project and strengthen the outcome.

You will measure all of your content against the synopsis that you write.

This applies to all nonfiction writing, including creative nonfiction. (Creative nonfiction involves writing from personal experience and/or reporting on other peoples' experiences – much like a reporter would do – but shaping it in a way that reads like fiction.) Develop a synopsis or storyline if you are writing fiction as well. Writers need some kind of map to keep them on the journey. However, recognize that characters within fiction can, and frequently do, take the storylines in directions not anticipated by the author. Often that new direction is the better way to go. Pay attention to your characters and revise your synopsis as necessary.

Now you need to describe your audience or market. To whom are you writing? Who will read your book? What is true for writing a synopsis holds for writing the description of your audience or market. Do not begin with "anyone who" or "anybody who," as that is a clear indication that you have not created a specific enough image of your audience.

Clearly defining your audience not only facilitates the writing adventure but also assists in developing your marketing plans.

Several years ago while in conversation with a potential client, I asked her to describe her audience. She answered, "All women from the age of 14 and up. I want to help keep them from going through the things that I went through."

I challenged her to be more specific. Such an age range was too broad from my perspective. Vocabulary and concepts used to convey messages for younger teens differ from what an author can effectively use for older teens and adult women.

Joe Colavito is Vice President for External Development at Wells Management Company in Atlanta, Georgia, and another one of my writing clients. Joe describes his *Jelly Donut Delight* as an adult parable and it is. That means the book is storylike in nature – think of the various parables found in holy writings or even Aesop's fables – but uses vocabulary that young children might not understand.

When Evelyn Blasi came to me for help in writing *A Guide to Divorce: From Someone Who's Been There*, she very definitely targeted women. She wrote with fervor to encourage women who did not necessarily want to be in divorce proceedings. Her words are strong, direct and helpful.

Clearly identifying or describing one's audience is particularly critical when writing for children. Many people mistakenly believe that writing for children is the easiest writing to engage in: just tell a good, fanciful story with a happy ending. Not so. From my perspective, writing for children is among the most difficult and challenging writing one can engage in because of language limitations. Can you remember the vocabulary lists we received when we were students in grade school? Those new words we were to learn each week to grow our vocabulary? There is a significant difference among word level and difficulty between each of the grade levels. Beginning writers tend to forget that.

An individual came to me once with eight children's stories in hand. He had told them time and again to his grandchildren. After much prodding from his daughter and grandchildren, he finally wrote out the stories. Would I look at them and critique them for him? My first question was, "What age range did you have in mind when you developed these stories?"

"Well, for my grandchildren," he quickly answered

"What are their ages?"

I don't remember what he said their ages were but the answer he gave me presented far too wide of an age range and I commented on that.

"But they like them. They enjoy them."

"I understand that," I told him. "But these are your grandchildren.

They are just thrilled to death that their grandpa is making up stories for them regardless of whether they fully understand them or not."

When I wrote *Letters to My Sons: a Father's Faith Journey*, I confronted an intriguing situation. I actually had two audiences: my sons and the general public. At the time I wrote the book, my sons were 22 and 18. I figured by the time I would get the book published they would be at least two years older (they were actually three years older by the time my book appeared; however, I had emailed them each letter as I finished writing it). I had to write to that level but I also had in mind the adult population who I believed would enjoy the book as well. That population is described in the last few lines of the book's synopsis (found on the back cover): ". . . *Letters to My Sons* presents the formation of a moderate to liberal theology. The book encourages readers to have serious, heart-felt, down-in-the-dirt conversations with God." In other words, I was writing to adults who were willing to wrestle with God over some significant faith issues.

Here is what you should consider when you define your audience/market:

1) Determine an age or age range;

2) Will your readers fall into a particular socio-economic group;

3) Describe where they live: their homes, their communities;

4) What activities would they most likely be engaged in;

Then consider any other information that you believe is relevant to helping you maintain focus in writing your manuscript.

Your next step prior to beginning to write your book is to create your initial table of contents. The synopsis and audience description provide a solid foundation to guide you in your writing. The table of contents can be more fluid, flexible, changing as you write.

If you used the mind mapping exercise discussed in the previous chapter, that map provides the basis for your table of contents as well as a beginning outline for writing. Perhaps you elected to generate a typical linear outline and you know which lines in the outline are your chapter titles. Use those lines for your initial table of contents. Remember you will eventually need additional entries: foreword, preface, introduction, acknowledgement, dedication. You can include those lines now or wait and enter them as you write. The key is simply to get a rough outline for your manuscript.

For now you might list the major topics you will discuss, or the themes or the movement of the plot of your novel. You are not necessarily giving titles to the chapters; you are "reserving space" for each chapter and determining the order in which you will discuss the material.

Now you are ready to begin your <u>first draft</u>. Remember that a first draft is a first draft. Your task is to write, keep your pen or pencil moving or your fingers active on the keyboard. Write as much as you can about each of your topics, themes or chapters. Don't worry about having too much information and do not concern yourself about proper flow, at least not yet. Simply focus on getting the first draft written. There will be a second, a third and maybe even a fourth draft before you are ready to consider publication. In each of those drafts you will become more critical of your content. You will watch for continuity and flow. For now your only task is to get it written.

I want to tell you about another practice that I use occasionally. Before you get too far into writing your manuscript, write your last sentence or closing paragraph. With nonfiction writing that should be fairly easy. With fiction, that could be a difficult challenge as you may only think you know the ending; your characters and the plot itself may lead you in a different direction.

By writing the last sentence or last paragraph, you have one more factor to guide you as you write. You know where you have to end up. All that you write has to eventually lead to this last sentence, this final paragraph.

I found that when I began imagining those final words and writing them down early in the stages of my essays, articles and books, my writing itself went more smoothly. If I started going off track, then I would consider whether my content had to be revised or whether it now had a different flow and needed a new ending.

How did I know if I had my ending? I could "hear" heavenly trumpets playing, "see" the Hollywood search lights scanning the sky, "hear" some magnificent symphony or a loud cymbal crash. Trust your instincts and your creative abilities. Write what you think will be your ending. Keep writing and revising until you hear or see something. Your mind will provide you with some image or sound. You will know. You have your tentative ending.

One last discussion before closing this chapter. Item seven in the query letter contents – the basis of your authority – may have given you cause for concern. Do not be intimidated by it. This does not mean you have to have college degrees or graduate degrees or formal education in order to write on a subject. What you do need in the area of nonfiction is something that clearly indicates you have a basis for writing about your topic. You may have worked in the profession or field for several years. You have done extensive research and have a bibliography to show for it. You write about your hobby, your family, your personal experience. Those each are a basis for authority. Approach this matter seriously. Publishers and readers want to know why they should devote their time and money to your book. Your basis for authority provides a reason.

Why does the Labyrinth attract people? Because it is a tool to guide healing, deepen self-knowledge, and empower creativity. ~ Dr. Lauren Artress from her book: *Walking a Sacred Path*

Do you have a labyrinth story to share? I want to hear it: **stories@writechoiceservices.com**. Subject: **labyrinth**

Basically, if you want to become a good writer, you need to do three things. Read a lot, listen well and deeply, and write a lot . . . ~ Natalie Goldberg

Chapter 9

Reading and Writing Go Together

If you want to be a writer, you must do two things above all others: read a lot and write a lot. ~ Stephen King

. . . becoming a better writer is going to help you become a better reader, and that is the real payoff. ~ Anne Lamott

Reading usually precedes writing. And the impulse to write is almost always fired by reading. Reading, the love of reading is what makes you dream of becoming a writer.
~ Susan Sontag

Reading and writing go together and even compete.
~ Ted Kooser & Steve Cox

    Think about the authors you enjoy reading. What is it about their writing that you like? Is it the way the author tells a story? Is it the manner in which the author uses words or even the words that the author elects to use? Does your enjoyment emerge from the things that the author writes about; things the author says? Maybe you like a particular author because of what the writer chooses *not* to say or do that other writers in that particular writing category do.

The next time you read an author whose writing you admire, don't just read but listen as well. If necessary, read aloud to yourself so that you will truly hear the writer's words. What sounds good in your head as you read? Is it the structure of sentences and paragraphs? Is it the words themselves? How about the rhythm that you hear in the words? The cadence in a paragraph?

And the next time you find yourself reading something that you don't like, read it aloud as well and ask yourself the same questions. Why don't the words sound good? What creates the dissonance? Is it the rhythm? Sentence or paragraph structure? Choice of words?

Reading helps us identify what we like and what we don't like in writing style. Awareness of both helps us discover how we want to write. As you approach writing your manuscript, you should be engaged in reading other books in the genre in which you intend to write. If you plan to write a memoir, read some memoirs. If you intend to write about your insight in business, find some similar type of business books and read them. Romance? Read romance. Travelogue? Read travelogue. Notice how each book is paced and how words are put together. You get the idea.

Kooser and Cox in *Writing Brave and Free* comment: "*Every* writer learns from imitation and the more you read the more you find to imitate to model your own work. Part of the discipline of writing is to read as much as you can. Reading helps you discern good writing from bad writing."

No one is suggesting that you copy another author's style. Rather, the intent is to allow the writing styles of the authors whom you enjoy to filter through your mind. When you write, your writing style will be your interpretation of the accumulation of styles that speak to you. What emerges is called your writing voice.

I want to share with you an experience that I think will help you understand the filtering concept. This happened in my middler year of seminary in a course on constructive theology. Dr. Bryant, our beloved theology professor, directed each of us students to choose a theologian who interested us, and then read a good selection of that theologian's writings. Through our reading we were to discern:

- what we believed to be the theologian's key points;
- how the theologian presented his/her arguments in written form;
- the flow of the writing/discussion.

When we completed that task (and we had about three weeks), we were to tackle a second theologian in a similar fashion. With the second theologian we did not need to read as much or dig as deeply. The purpose of becoming familiar with a second theologian was to have a basis for comparison. Did each of them emphasize the same elements of theology? How did their writing impact us? Was it heavy and ponderous? Or did we find the writing to be easily read and understood? What did we like about what they shared, how they wrote, and as such, their treatment of the reader?

Once we had completed the comparison, our final task – literally – was to write the beginnings of our personal theology. In writing our theological statement, we would draw upon what we had learned, "heard," and experienced in our journey through the writings of two different theologians. Then we would offer the beginnings of our own theology: our understanding of God, creation and whatever other theological tenet we felt compelled to discuss.

This process, which I went through to generate an initial personal theological statement, is what writers do on a regular basis. We read the works of those whose writings we enjoy. We compare the styles of those authors – consciously or subconsciously – and then generate our own way of writing.

Engaging in reading helps our writing in other ways. Francine Prose's *Reading Like a Writer: a Guide for People Who Love Books and for Those Who Want to Write Them* provides a passionate, humorous and insightful look into the tools and tricks of writing masters. Prose helps us understand why their writings have endured and what we can learn from them. Her book made it onto the New York Times Best-Sellers list.

Prose suggests that a good writing seminar or writing class should have as a companion course a reading course that focuses on the masters of writing. Courses, classes and seminars tell us what we are doing wrong, what we are doing poorly, what we need to change, and what we neglected to do. Knowing all the things that we have done wrong does not necessarily bring us any closer to understanding what we ought to do. Reading selections from the pens of great writers provides that piece. In the writings and words of Shakespeare, Jane Austen, Charles Dickens, Charlotte Bronte, Stephen Crane, Ernest Hemingway, William Faulkner, Eudora Welty or Toni Morrison, we witness how brilliantly words can come together. We see how ideas are crafted and themes are developed. Their writings challenge us and inspire us.

In the chapter "Reading for Courage," Prose points out, "Reading can give you the courage to resist all of the pressures that our culture exerts on you to write in a certain way, or to follow a prescribed form. It can even persuade you that it might not be necessary to give your novel or story a happy ending."

Francine Prose speaks the obvious, which is not necessarily all that obvious. She reminds us that we build our writing around words and then sentences and then paragraphs. Obviously – but do we really take that in as we write? Many of the emerging writers whom I encounter "have a book they have to get written." I understand that, but it helps to begin the journey of writing by looking at words as they develop into sentences and then into paragraphs.

If we plan to write and to be taken seriously with our writing, then we must understand the discipline of writing, which is actually quite simple: we write and then we write, and then we write, and then we write some more. Then we re-write. Writing, good writing, demands that eventually we study, ponder, cogitate – call it what you will – the best work, the best phrase that we can generate in all of our writing. And of course we have to be ready to cut. And we can cut out a lot of verbiage.

All of these thoughts are why writers read. We read the works of our favorite writers. We read books in the genre in which we write. We read to hear the sound of other writers. We read in order to explore the subtle structures and styles of other writers. We read to learn. We read to become better at our craft.

But . . . the book you want to write is the only book you ever intend to write so why go through all of this reading stuff? Because, if you want your writing to be taken seriously by your readers, your intended readers, then your book needs to have the sound (voice) that is similar to other writers of the genre in which you will be writing. When your style of writing and the sound of your writing reflect other writers in your genre, your credibility automatically increases. That is very important.

Back in the 1980s the Kellogg Company introduced a new advertising campaign for Kellogg's Corn Flakes with the tag line: Taste them again for the first time. Tweak that tag line a bit and you have a concise description of what a writer is about – we try ideas again for the first time. We realize that we have a different way of doing something that has been done the same way "forever." What we write challenges people to look at something again for the first time, to experience something again for the first time. As writers, we put our interpretation on an event, an idea, a process, an experience and we ask our readers to "try it again for the first time."

Writing and reading go together. It is not just that we write and others read what we write. Rather, we as writers need to read as well. And if you have any doubt about that, re-read the five quotes at the beginning of the chapter. Those quotes from noteworthy and successful writers share the writers' perspective on reading.

From American author and McIntosh Professor of English at Barnard College Mary Gordon, comes this comment on writing and reading. I offer it as a most appropriate summation on reading and writing:

The greatest and cheapest university – where great teachers abound, the classes are free and there's never any crowding – is just a library card away. Reading, most writers agree, is the best teacher.

What books have helped you with your writing? These may be books on writing or simply books that you have read that you know gave you insight on voice or style or content or anything significant to your writing. Share those book titles and authors with me: **stories@writechoiceservices.com.** Subject line: **reading and writing**.

What I am trying to achieve is a voice sitting by a
fireplace telling you a story on a winter's evening.
~ *Truman Capote*

Chapter 10

Finding Your Writing Voice

Much of what was shared in the previous chapter on reading and writing applies to this discussion on "writing voice" and your being able to discover your writing voice. We talked about what appeals to your ear when you read an author's writing and what does not. We spoke of sentence structure and word choice and the development of paragraphs and dialogue. All of these combine to create "voice" – your voice – the voice of the writer.

You may not have thought about voice as you prepare to write. But you do have a sense of voice. Think of the authors whom you enjoy reading. You like the way they write or tell a story – you like their voice. You are comfortable with their writing.

In *Finding Your Voice: How to Put Personality in Your Writing,* Les Edgerton shares this bit of whimsical information: "Someone with far too much time on his/her hands once counted how many different words Hemingway used in all of his writings (books, stories, articles). The total was 8,000." Imagine using only 8,000 different words to create all the pages of writing that Hemingway authored. That suggests to me that Hemingway knew his audience. He knew who they were or who he intended the audience to be and he recognized what words would speak and what words might detract. He had a clear understanding of his writing voice.

Recognizing your writing voice has probably not been a concern. During our high school and college days, when we tackled our writing assignments, our focus was not on finding a voice or on setting our papers apart from others in the class by our use of words and sentences. We wrote to meet what we believed were the desires and demands of the teacher or professor. We did the research, created an outline, and wrote a first draft. Then we edited and reworked the draft, polished it up and submitted a well-reasoned argument substantiating our point of view. Meeting the teachers' standards and attaining a respectable grade influenced whatever writing voice we had. In the process, we may have lost our natural writing voice. That is assuming that we had one to begin with. We probably did, but because of our experiences in writing, our writing voice might be best described as beige.

How might you find your voice as you set about to write? One way to begin is to look at your writing: letters you have written to family and friends, journal entries, diaries, reflections. There is a good chance you will see hints of your writing voice. Is there a pattern or rhythm to your writing? Can you feel a cadence within the words? Do you use more one syllable words or more multi-syllable words or a good mixture? Your answers guide you in recognizing your writing voice.

Barry Holstun Lopez, author, essayist, and fiction writer, describes writing as not so much concerned with showing how smart you are but about telling the best story you know, the best way you can.

Tell your story in the best way you can. That is important. Writing is not about how you think a story should be told. Writing is not about how others think you should tell your story. Writing is about the best way in which you can tell your story – whatever that story may be. It is using your own voice.

How do you strengthen your voice? Through practice. You write and write and write and critique your writing. Read it aloud to yourself and listen; truly listen. How does it sound? Does what you have read sound solid? Is there a flow to it, or does it sound stiff, stilted? Keep at it. Keep writing whatever you want to write: general reflections, a short story, a chapter in your manuscript, general musings. Write. Read aloud. Listen. Critique and write some more. Keep at it.

Those whom I coach get tripped up in discovering their writing voice because they work from their head and ignore their heart. Your true writing voice and solid writing emerge when you find the critical balance between what your head thinks should be written and what your heart believes should be written. When I think about that balance, I literally envision the throat, which is roughly midpoint between your head (brain) and your heart.

If your writing is too centered in your head, then it may be difficult to understand or sound stiff, dry. If you center your writing too much in your heart, then your words may sound light weight, too emotional. You want to find a balance, and out of that balance your voice will emerge.

Throughout *Reading Like a Writer: a Guide for People Who Love Books and for Those Who Want to Write Them,* Prose encourages writers to hold onto an adventurous spirit when writing. I also hear a call to find your own authentic writing voice, the one that does indeed reside within you – not that beige voice you used when you wrote essays and term papers.

One of the best ways to avoid a beige voice is in just being yourself as you write. Allow your writing voice to reflect the way that you speak. Yes, you may have to tighten it up a bit: get rid of slang and fillers (um, ah, like, cool, etc.) None the less, one of the secrets to good writing is to write as you speak. That is your voice. In the previous chapter – Reading and Writing Go Together – I discussed how we find ourselves drawn to particular authors because of their voice. Your readers will be drawn to you for a similar reason: they enjoy your voice.

Just be yourself! How often did we hear that advice from our parents during our school days? We worried about being liked by our classmates, having friends, being accepted. If we screwed up our courage to share our anxiety with our parents that was when they told us: "Just be yourself and people will like you." We wanted to believe them but it seemed too simple. Well, the same advice holds in writing – just be yourself. Write in your natural voice.

In *Finding Your Voice,* Les Edgerton provides guidelines, advice and a lot of exercises for recognizing and developing your own unique and natural writing voice. One hint of what you will discover in his book should you choose to read it is: One technique for voice is not so much to go outside the self, but rather to go deep inside for what already resides there, bringing to the writing desk the same techniques that talented actors employ.

Do what actors do . . . I called Mike Pniewski, actor, friend, and client. Mike has worked successfully as an actor for over 20 years. He has worked with some of the biggest stars in the world –Tom Hanks, Denzel Washington, Mel Brooks, Gene Hackman, Helen Mirren, and dozens more. He has appeared in almost 40 movies including: *Miami Vice; Ray; Bobby Jones-Stroke of Genius; The Clearing; Runaway Jury; A Time to Kill;* and *Beverly Hills Cop.* Mike's TV credits include *CSI: Miami, Law & Order, ER, Boston Public, The Fugitive,* and *Drop Dead Diva.*

I shared Edgerton's quote with Mike and then asked, "What is the technique that talented actors employ?"

Mike laughed as he usually does several times during any conversation that we have. Then he began to reflect. What follows, I wrote from my notes of that conversation:

"So often in life and in many ways, we try to live up to the expectations of others; to do what we think others want us to do. That can be disastrous, especially for an actor. An actor must always remember the audience. The audience and the director want to hear my truth, my experience, my passion.

"When I play a role, I bring to that role my own point of view from my own life experience. I bring that role to life based upon a life that is real. Being an effective actor goes deeper than being talented. The actor has to speak from a place where things matter and that is from deep inside the self. An actor works to create originality, life in the moment if you will. An actor must have a real deep level of trust in the self in order to speak his or her own truth, experience and passion. An actor must trust the self and believe that he or she is giving enough and giving in an honest and passionate way."

Mike then told of an audition he once had. He had read through the script four or five times. His reaction was that he just didn't fit the role: that of a guy strung out on PCP, an addict with a serious problem. But Mike went in for the audition anyway and when he got there, he discovered that he was the only male that the director had asked to see.

Mike began to think, "Why am I here? Why me? What is it that I do well?" And he knew the answer: "I do my own truth well and that is what the director wanted. He wanted my truth and knew I would express it – not the truth that I might think or the audience would expect to be the image of a middle-aged guy, unkempt, long hair, a bit odorous, strung out on PCP." Mike proceeded to nail the audition.

If we as writers emulate actors in finding and expressing our voice, then we go deep inside ourselves to find our truth, to own the experiences that have shaped our view of the world, to tap into our passion. A theme of this book is that writers bring to the world their own, individual, and unique perspectives on the world: on their family, on processes or procedures in work, a creative work of fiction. We bring that unique view only when we write with our own voice – not the voice that we think others want us to use. Go deep inside. Find your truth. Write about your truth. Write about your experience. Be bold.

Declare, "This is who I am. This is how I view the world. This is how I tell a story."

Use your voice, your writing voice.

By all means stay away from beige!

(If you would like to know more about Mike Pniewski and how he uses his knowledge of acting to help others in their careers, visit his website *www.throwemback.com*.)

It is solved by walking. ~St. Augustine

If you are struggling with finding your voice, this would be a great time to enter a labyrinth.

A writer's job is to make the ordinary come alive, to awaken ourselves to the specialness of simply being.

~ Natalie Goldberg

Chapter 11

Writing as an Act of Discovery, Reverence & Sacred Trust

Writers write because we have something to share: an experience, a unique bit of knowledge, an interesting story, a professional insight, or perhaps words of encouragement. Writers have a relationship with the topic about which we write. We have lived it, experienced it, or, maybe, dreamed it. Whatever the motivation or whatever the "it" may be, that which we write about is part of who we are, even an element of our belief system.

My assumption is that you understand those thoughts. Even now, an ember glows within you of something you must write. The ember yearns to burst into a flame of creativity. The flame intensifies once you begin to write. As you write, odds are very good that you will discover new ideas or themes or possibilities for your writing topic. Your journey is underway.

Writing is an act of discovery. The writer does not set out to generate a new dictionary entry or encyclopedia article. Rather the writer seeks to share the journey of awareness. This is what I have learned because . . . This is what I experienced when . . . I have always done the process this way, then one day I decided to do something different and . . . This story came to my mind; the more I thought about it, the more it took shape. And here it is . . .

You are poised to begin your act of discovery. This is your journey of awareness and you will choose your words wisely so that you convey your ideas clearly. Through your words and details you invite others to join in your journey of discovery. As you write, you declare, "This is what I know to be true. I share this with you, the reader, so that you might learn from my life lesson, my life experience, from the creative imaginations of my mind."

This book discloses one of my journeys of discovery. Being a writer, a published author, a writing coach was not a part of any vision that I held for myself as a child or teenager planning for my future. I remember the red ink syndrome in my life and I rejoiced mightily when I finished Freshmen English Composition in college. I knew I wasn't done with writing, as there would always be term papers and research papers to generate as long as I was an undergraduate and graduate student. But those papers would be written on topics of my own choosing, not from the "obviously dark recesses of some teacher's or professor's mind." That writing I looked forward to.

I entered ministry and came face to face with a truth that I knew but had not fully contemplated. There is this thing called a weekly sermon; in the secular/business world one would call it an essay or column. The basis for that weekly essay was a story that the people to whom I would speak, for whom I had written, knew very well already. I had to tell them something new, different, exciting, relevant, yet true to the source and maintain their interest. Now that is a challenge. That is an amazing training ground for writing!

Each week was an adventure, an act of discovery. What would I find new, different, or relevant? What will I learn? How can I share the discovery so that I hold the listeners' attention (or the readers' as well, since my sermons were printed and available).

You are in business. You have developed processes that work for you. You have taken the standard operating procedures and tweaked them into something that works really well for you, for your company. Now the time has come for you to write about it so that you can clarify your own thinking and understanding and share it with others. You engage in an act of discovery.

Reading through some family diaries or looking through photo albums, you learn things about your family that you didn't know. Or you gain a new perspective on a family secret. You want to share; but what if other family members challenge your interpretation of things? So you hesitate to write. Write anyway. Engage in that act of discovery.

Over the past few years, my sister and I have had many fascinating telephone conversations. Our parents died 21 and 16 years ago. Our brother died when he was 33. When we talk, we reminisce. We laugh. We challenge. How does it happen that we had the same parents, grew up in the same house, attended the same family gatherings and have uniquely different viewpoints? It all comes down to how my sister and I interpreted the people and the events, based upon what was important to us and how we each felt about the people, the situation, and our attitude at the time. Our truth, though differing in many ways, remains true because the truth emerges from our unique act of discovery in looking at and reflecting upon our family history.

If you hunger to write a memoir or some kind of family history but hesitate because some of the ideas you have shared with family have led them to question the events or brought reflections contradicting your reflections, hesitate no longer. Write! In writing you share your personal take on the world.

Maybe it is a work of fiction that you dream of writing. You have begun your act of discovery – created initial character descriptions, have a rough plot. You tell a friend of your idea and your friend reminds you of at least one book, if not more, with a similar theme. Don't panic! Above all, don't quit. Writers assume no new plots or themes exist; all have been used at sometime in history. The task of a writer is to take a plot or theme and make it her own. When you write, you bring your understanding, your perspective – your "truth." That makes it all unique.

I included Natalie Goldberg's comment at the top of the chapter because she speaks to this issue, to make the ordinary come alive. We make the ordinary come alive in our writing as we share our view of the world around us.

It is from Anne Lamott that I have taken the perspective that writing is an act of reverence. "I honestly think in order to be a writer, you have to learn to be reverent. If not, why are you writing? Why are you here?" writes Lamott in *Bird by Bird*. She adds, "Let's think of reverence as awe, as presence in and openness to the world."

The reverence already exists as we prepare to write; our challenge is not to lose that reverence. We are awed with an idea. Amazement grips us as we recognize that what we do in our professional life is a little different from others who share the same profession, and that difference makes all the difference in the world. We visit family cemetery plots and discover that Uncle Walt was a major in the US Army in both World War II and Korea and no one, not even Uncle Walt, ever talked about that. We only knew that he never wrote his PhD dissertation so he never received his PhD and that he was an alcoholic who never dried out. But he was a major and he was a scholar – awe, grounded in reverence, creeps into our heart. How can we learn more about him?

Remember the excitement that came over you when you learned . . . recognized . . . realized? Do you remember how that excitement turned to awe and then reverence? As writers, we need to maintain that reverence as we write. If we lose the sense of reverence, most likely our writing will become dull maybe even meaningless. Our words will no longer have the impact they might have carried. Maintain reverence toward your writing,

Regardless of the genre, writing is grounded in sacred trust. A relationship exists between the reader and the writer: the reader trusts that the writer will express something of value; that reading the writer's words will be a worthwhile endeavor. An unspoken sacred trust exists.

Earlier, I wrote of the importance of identifying one's audience or market as a critical step at the beginning of the writing process. That identity provides a focus for your writing. That identity provides the foundation for the sacred trust; for you, as the writer, must always maintain respect for your reader and hold your reader in high regard. Ultimately, you give your best to your reader. You do your part to create, build and maintain the sacred trust you have with your readers.

Clearly this sacred trust concept pertains to any writing that you intend to present to the world. The writing that you do for yourself – everyday general writing, journaling, or whatever form it takes – you need not hold to such a high level. You may not even want to be reverent in those daily writing adventures. But I do urge you always to view as an act of discovery any writing that you do, whether of the daily "grind" type or writing you do for public consumption.

Writing as an act of discovery, reverence and sacred trust never entered our minds during our school days, when our focus was on limiting the amount of red ink we would find on our essays, themes, and term papers. We wrote according to the rules of grammar and to the standards or guidelines established by our teacher, the professor or the nature of the project. Our head managed that writing and made sure that we adhered to the rules. Minimal amounts of what we wrote surfaced from the heart.

In the writing that you hunger to engage in now, it is absolutely critical that your heart be in play. Grammar rules still apply because the universal understanding of the rules of grammar enables people to read and understand the written word. And there are the rules that apply to genres. But now your heart must be present in your writing. Even technical writing should have an element of heart in it. By keeping your heart engaged as you write, then reverence and sacred trust will be present as well.

William Zinsser offers these thoughts in *On Writing Well*: "Writing is related to character. If your values are sound, you writing will be sound. It all begins with intention. Figure out what you want to do and how you want to do it, and work your way with humanity and integrity to the completed [writing project]."

From Elizabeth Gilbert, author of *Eat, Pray, Love*, comes this challenge: "I believe that – if you are serious about a life of writing, or indeed about any creative form of expression – that you should take on this work like a holy calling."

Writing is indeed an act of discovery, reverence and sacred trust.

I have a keen interest in hearing your thoughts on and experiences with writing as an act of discovery, reverence and sacred trust. Please share your thoughts with me. E-mail me at: **stories@writechoiceservices.com.** Use the word **sacred** in the subject line.

I have never thought of myself as a good writer. Anyone who wants reassurance of that should read one of my first drafts. But I'm one of the world's great re-writers. ~ James Michener

Chapter 12

Now to Begin

I delight in Michener's words. James Michener is the author of the best-selling books *Hawaii, Tales of the South Pacific, Sayonara, Chesapeake, The Covenant, Alaska, The Drifters, The Bridges at Toko-Ri.* This is what writing is all about: writing and then re-writing and re-writing and maybe even re-writing some more. And the time has arrived for you to begin that journey.

In this book, I have helped you recognize ghosts from papers we have written in the past that subconsciously keep us from writing today. We know that all those years we spent writing themes and essays and term papers to meet a teacher's expectations have probably crippled our creativity but now that we know it, we can move beyond it. Concurrent with those memories is the red ink syndrome. Those papers that we wrote to meet a teacher's expectations more than likely came back to us graded and covered with corrections and comments made in red ink. We remember that red ink. But we can move beyond it.

You have learned how to use *lectio divina* to identify your book topic and also how to use mind mapping to generate an outline or to fine tune the search for a specific writing topic.

In the last three chapters I shared with you the impact reading can and does have on writing and how reading helps the writer discover his/her writing voice. Then I ventured to suggest that writing is an act of discovery, reverence and sacred trust. In that chapter I challenged you to see more deeply into the act of writing and what writing offers to you and to your readers.

From my perspective, the time has arrived for you to write your manuscript/book. It is time to get to work. I want to share some random thoughts pertinent to the journey you are about to commence.

1) As you engage in research for your writing, you will be tempted to consult one more book, read one more article, talk to one more person. There will always be "one more something" you could do. Recognize that; and when you do, tell yourself: Enough! And start writing.

2) Three comments from Elizabeth Gilbert, author of *Eat, Pray, Love*, from her article entitled "Some thoughts on Writing:"

   a) Your job is only to write your heart out, and let destiny take care of the rest;

   b) Writing is not like dancing or modeling; it's not something where – if you missed it by age 19 – you're finished. It's never too late. Your writing will only get better as you get older and wiser.

   c) Nobody can tell you how to succeed at writing (even if they write a book called "How to Succeed at Writing") because there is no WAY; there are, instead, many ways.

3) In line with Gilbert's last comment, find what works for you. Check out all of the how-to-write books in your local bookstore or one of the national book retail stores or Amazon.com or any other online book store. You could be overwhelmed with the number of books on writing. (And now there is one more: this one!) Choose the ones that intrigue you. Read through them, learn from them, but use only the processes or ideas that make sense to you, that speak to your heart and head.

4) If you are serious about being a writer, then practice – which means write and write and write.

5) MFA (masters of fine arts degree) students write a minimum of 18 hours/week so if you want to be a writer of some note . . . you may not be able to write that many hours each week but you do need to be writing.

6) You don't necessarily need huge blocks of time; use even spare moments – Ben Hamper wrote his best-selling book *Rivetheads* during coffee and lunch breaks on the production line and in the evenings.

7) Don't set up a writing system and blindly adhere to it; use it as a guideline.

8) Even in practice writing, write about the truth as you see it or experience it.

9) Don't underestimate the importance and power of simply sitting down at your desk and writing: "gluing" yourself to your desk chair and writing.

10) When you need encouragement, read stories from *Chicken Soup for the Writer's Soul: Stories to Open the Heart and Rekindle the Spirit of Writers*.

11) Good writing emerges from a balance between writing from the head and writing from the heart.

12) Go deep inside. Find your truth. Write about your truth. Write about your experience. Be bold.

And take to heart Michener's comment: "I have never thought of myself as a good writer. . . . But I'm one of the world's great re-writers."

All writers are re-writers.

Appendix

Labyrinth Resources

BOOKS

Artress, Lauren, *Walking a Sacred Path: Rediscovering the Labyrinth as a Sacred Tool*, New York: Riverhead Books, 1995

West, Melissa Gayle, *Exploring the Labyrinth: A Guide for Healing and Spiritual Growth*, New York: Broadway Books, 2000

Westbury, Virginia, *Labyrinths: Ancient Paths of Wisdom and Peace*, DeCapo Press, 2001

WEBSITES

There are literally tens of thousands of possible websites to view or read concerning labyrinths. I list the three that I use most frequently. Each of these provides additional information on the history of labyrinths, search engines to locate labyrinths, and much more.

www.labyrinthsociety.org

www.labyrinths.org

www.lessons4living.com/labyrinth.htm

Should you wish to purchase a pocket labyrinth or any labyrinth products, I recommend that you type into your search engine of choice – pocket labyrinth – and choose from the myriad options.

The Chartres Labyrinth

The Cretan Labyrinth

Guidelines for Walking the Labyrinth

- Choose which of the 2 labyrinths you want to walk.

- Determine your purpose for the journey.

- Enter the labyrinth with a clear purpose.

- Walk the path at a speed you desire. You may even choose to vary your speed.

- Stop along the way if you wish – to ponder, reflect, rest.

- Upon reaching the center you may elect to remain in the center for awhile to meditate, think about what has come to your mind in your walk so far, or you may decide to begin immediately the journey back out.

- The same suggestions apply to the journey out as with the journey in: walk at a speed you desire, vary your speed if you wish, stop along the way if you want to.

- Just before leaving the labyrinth, pause for a moment to reflect on what you heard or experienced in your walk.

- Take note of the clarity that has come to your mind.

Mind Map

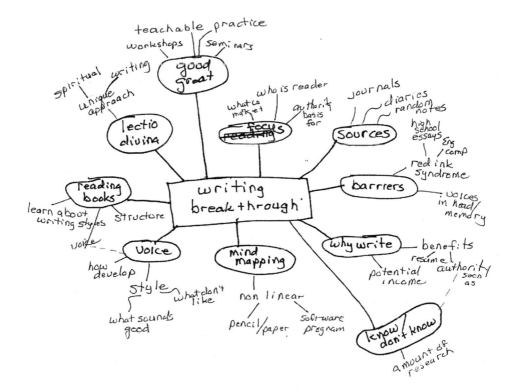

Magazines for Writers

There are many magazines written and published just for writers. An internet search will uncover many of them. The four listed below are easily found in major bookstores. These are the ones that I read consistently and recommend to my clients. I have included the websites for each magazine as well. The individual websites offer a wealth of information and additional resources.

Poets & Writers Magazine *www.pw.org/mag* is the magazine "arm" of Poets & Writers, Inc., a nonprofit, tax-exempt corporation organized for literary and education purposes. It is the nation's largest nonprofit organization serving creative writers.

The Writer *www.writermag.com* From the website, describes itself as ". . .full of features you can use to improve your writing, including before-and-after examples of improved writing, more literary markets than ever before, practical solutions for writing problems, selected literary magazine profiles, tips from famous authors and hands-on advice."

Writer's Digest *www.writersdigest.com* From the website, describes itself as ". . . [bringing] you the must-know tips and publishing secrets you'll need such as: technique articles geared toward specific genres; business information specifically for writers; tips and tricks for rekindling your creative spark; inspirational stories of writers who are living the dream, and how they got there; the latest . . . markets for print, online and e-publishing; tools of the trade, including the latest advice and info on software, books and Web resources."

WRITERS' Journal *www.writersjournal.com* From the website describes itself as "The Complete Writer's Magazine . . . directed toward all writers. [A] blend of poetry, prose, photography helps, screenwriting hints, marketing aids, editing advice, and the opportunity to be published . . ."

Helpful and Informative Websites for Writers

This list includes the author's websites and a variety of other websites to which the author has turned for information, insight and inspiration.

www.writechoiceservices.com The website for Tim Morrison's writing company; share your questions with Tim and the writers who help in coaching other writers.

www.yourwriteresource.com Tim has partnered with Brownell Landrum and Jay Scott to provide a "one-stop" resource for writers who want help in writing, in developing a website and in using social media to promote themselves and their work

follow Tim Morrison on twitter **@wecoachwriting**

www.writingthewhirlwind.com Website for author and writing coach Jill Jepson.

www.CarolineJoyAdams.com Website for author, speaker and writing coach Caroline Joy Adams.

www.writingfix.com Designed for teachers, students and writers; provides interactive prompts, lessons, and resources for writing classrooms seeks to show that writing, especially in a class room setting can be fun.

www.Bartleby.com Great Books on line; read segments from great literature, find quotes.

www.copyright.gov US copyright office; all the information you need concerning copyrights

www.grammarbook.com Good source for grammar and punctuation; free online English usage rules

www.sfwa.org/beware Provides warnings about the schemes, scams and pitfalls that threaten writers.

www.easywaytowrite.com/articles.html An extensive collection of a variety of articles on writing

www.writersweekly.com Books, articles, markets, warnings and more in an ezine format

www.emergingwriters.typepad.com The EWN was created to develop a community of emerging writers, established writers deserving of wider recognition, and readers of literary writing, in order to develop as large an audience as possible for those writers.

www.enhancemywriting.com A collection of indispensible writing resources

www.newbiewriters.com For new writers, would-be writers, aspiring writers and beginner writers of all genres and from all walks of life.

www.writerunboxed.com Information and articles about the craft and business of genre fiction.

www.writing-tipstoday.com Articles on writing, writing checklists, resources.

www.authonomy.com A new community site for writers, readers and publishers, conceived and developed by book editors at HarperCollins.

www.nanowrimo.org Website for the National Novel Writing Month (November)

www.writing-world.com Compendium of articles, blogs, information on all aspects of writing and genres

www.aminstitute.com Check out the headline analyzer tab to see how strong your book title or article title is.

Bibliography

Bennett, Hal Zina, *Writing Spiritual Books: A Bestselling Writer's Guide to Successful Publication*, San Francisco: Inner Ocean Publishing, Inc., 2004

Bowerman, Peter, *The Well-Fed Writer: Financial Self-Sufficiency as a Freelance Writer in Six Months or Less*, Atlanta: Fanove Publishing, 2001

Bowerman, Peter, *The Well-Fed Writer: Back for Seconds: A Second Helping of "How-To" for Any Writer Dreaming of Great Bucks and Exceptional Quality of Life*, Atlanta: Fanove Publishing, 2005

Canfield, Jack and Mark Victor Hansen and Bud Gardner, *Chicken Soup for the Writer's Soul: Stories to Open the Heart and Rekindle the Spirit of Writers*, Deerfield Beach, FL: Health Communications, Inc., 2000

Clark, Roy Peter, *Writing Tools: 50 Essential Strategies for Every Writer*, New York: Little, Brown and Company, 2006

Edgerton, Les, *Finding Your Voice: How to Put Personality in Your Writing*, Cincinnati, OH: Writer's Digest Books, 2003

Fletcher, Ralph, *A Writer's Notebook: Unlocking the Writer within You*, New York: HarperCollins, 2010

Freedom Writers, *The Freedom Writers Diary with Erin Gruwell: How a Teacher and 150 Teens Used Writing to Change Themselves and the World Around Them*, New York: Broadway Books, 1999

George, Elizabeth, *Write Away: One Novelist's Approach to Fiction and the Writing Life*, New York: HarperCollins, 2004

Going on Faith: Writing as a Spiritual Quest, William Zinsser, ed., New York: Marlowe and Company, 1999

Goldberg, Natalie, *Old Friend from Far Away: the Practice of Writing Memoir*, New York: Freedom Press, 2007

Goldberg, Natalie, *Writing Down the Bones: Freeing the Writer Within*, Boston: Shambhala, 1986

Grason, Sandy, *Journalution: Journaling to Awaken Your Inner Voice, Heal Your Life and Manifest Your Dreams*, Novato, California: New World Library, 2005

Hart, Jack, *A Writer's Coach: An Editor's Guide to Words that Work*, New York: Pantheon, 2006

Jepson, Jill, *Writing as a Sacred Path: A Practical Guide to Writing with Passion and Purpose*, Berkley: Celestial Arts, 2008

King, Stephen, *On Writing: a Memoir of the Craft*, New York: Scribner, 2000

Kooser, Ted and Steve Cox, *Writing Brave and Free: Encouraging Words for People Who Want to Start Writing*, Lincoln, NB: University of Nebraska Press, 2006

Kremer, John, *1001 Ways to Market Your Books: for Authors and Publishers* – 4th Edition, Fairfield, IA: Open Horizons, 1993

Lamott, Anne, *Bird by Bird: Some Instructions on Writing and Life*, New York: Anchor Books, 1994

Levine, Mark, *The Fine Print of Self-Publishing: The Contracts and Services of 45 Self-Publishing Companies – Analyzed, Ranked and Exposed*, Third Edition, Minneapolis: Bascom Hill Publishing Group, 2008

McIndoo, Ann, *So, You Want to Write!: How to Get Your Book Out of Your Head and Onto the Paper in 7 Days*, Charleston, SC: Elevate, 2006

Niles, Elaura, *Some Writers Deserve to Starve!: 31 Brutal Truths about the Publishing Industry*, Cincinnati, OH: Writer's Digest Books, 2005

Pipher, Mary, *Writing to Change the World*, New York: Riverhead Books, 2006

Prose, Francine, *Reading Like a Writer: a Guide for People Who Love Books and for Those Who Want to Write Them*, New York: Harper Perennial, 2006

Poynter, Dan, *Self-Publishing Manual: How to Write, Print and Sell Your Own Book* 15th Edition, Santa Barbara, CA: Para Publishing, 2006

Poynter, Dan, *Writing Nonfiction: Turning Thoughts into Books* Fourth Edition, Santa Barbara, CA: Para Publishing, 2005

Saltzman, Jocl, *If You Can Talk, You Can Write: a Proven Program to Get You Writing and Keep You Writing*, New York: Warner Books, 1993

Selling, Barnard, *Writing from Within: a Guide to Creativity and Life Story Writing*, New York: Barnes & Noble, 1998

Strunk, Jr., William and White, E.B., *The Elements of Style* – Third Edition, Boston: Allyn and Bacon, 1979

Truss, Lynne, *Eats, Shoots & Leaves: The Zero Tolerance Approach to Punctuation*, New York: Gotham Books 2004

White, Fred D., PhD., *Life Writing: Drawing from Personal Experience to Create Features You Can Publish*, Sanger, California: Quill Driver Books, 2004

Writers on Writing, Jon Winokur, ed., Philadelphia: Running Press, 1986

Writing it Right! How Successful Children's Authors Revise and Sell Their Stories, Sandy Asher, ed.,West Redding, Connecticut: Writer's Institute Publications, 2009

Zinsser, William, *On Writing Well: the Classic Guide to Writing Nonfiction* 7th Edition, New York: Collins, 2006

Zinsser, William, *Writing About Your Life: a Journey into the Past*, Philadelphia: De Capo Press, 2004

Zinsser, William, *Writing Places: the Life Journey of a Writer and Teacher*, New York: Harper, 2009

If you want to start writing,
you have to start.

About the Author
Tim Morrison

Tim Morrison is owner and president of Write Choice Services, Inc. and a writer and writing coach. He coaches individuals who have always wanted to write a book "someday." Prior to joining the staff of Write Choice Services, and, subsequently, buying the company, Tim served over 25 years in ministry.

Photo by Lisa M. Zunzanyika

Tim earned his doctor of ministry degree from Andover Newton Theological School and his doctor of naturopathy degree from Trinity College of Natural Health. Tim and his wife, Marta, live in Marietta, Georgia. They have two adult sons, Joel and Sean, and a daughter-in-law, Katie.

www.WriteChoiceServices.com

Quick Order Form
Satisfaction guaranteed

❑ **Email orders:** info@writechoiceservices.com

❑ **Telephone orders:** Call 1(678) 464 6702
Have your credit card ready.

❑ **Postal orders:**
Please send the Books. I understand that I may return any of them
for a full refund — for any reason, no questions asked.

Name:

Address:

City, State/Province, Postal Code

Tel:

Email:

Sales tax *(orders shipped to GA)*:

Payment Credit card: • Visa • MasterCard • Optima • AMEX • Discover

Card number:

Name on card: Exp. date:

Payment by Check, mail to: Write Choice Services
PMB 240 - 101 3605 Sandy Plains Rd
Marietta, GA 30066

See our web site for FREE information on:
Other books, Speaking/Seminars, Mailing lists, Consulting.

www.WriteChoiceServices.com